Language Study

in Middle School, High School, and Beyond

John S. Simmons
Florida State University
Tallahassee, Florida, USA

Lawrence Baines
Berry College
Mount Berry, Georgia, USA

Editors

International Reading Association
800 Barksdale Road, PO Box 8139
Newark, Delaware 19714-8139, USA

Copyright 1998 by the International Reading Association, Inc.
All rights reserved. No part of this publication may be reproduced or transmitted in any form or by any means, electronic or mechanical, including photocopy, or any informational storage and retrieval system, without permission from the publisher.

Library of Congress Cataloging in Publication Data
    Language study in middle school, high school, and beyond / John S. Simmons, Lawrence Baines, editors.
        p.   cm.
    Includes bibliographical references and index.
    1. Language arts (Middle school)—United States.   2. Language arts (Secondary)—United States.   3. Language experience approach in education—United States.   I. Simmons, John S.   II. Baines, Lawrence.
LB1631.L253   1998
428'.0071'2—dc21   97-39591
ISBN 0-87207-182-0

CONTENTS

*L*anguage Study in Middle School, High School, and Beyond is an important and timely addition to the International Reading Association's book list for at least two compelling reasons: the first deals with the audience, the second with substance. In the midst of the "great debate" of the 1960s—turned into open warfare in the 1990s—over how young children should learn to read and write, the importance of language and literacy learning has been obscured, if not marginalized, in English-speaking societies. There is little public urgency expressed for the language needs of older learners—not in the popular media, not in legislatures or departments of education, and not, I dare say, in professional organizations such as IRA. Yet, as this fine collection of work attests, language learning is as critical among adolescents and adults as it is among young children. To neglect one audience at the expense of another makes little sense educationally, socially, politically, or economically.

Language and learning are inextricably connected to each other in ways that make the uses to which we put language the center of the curriculum. As I read the page proofs of the book I was reminded of Douglas Barnes's insightful views on language and learning in *From Communication to Curriculum* (1992). Barnes observed not only that language is a major means by which people learn, but that what people learn can hardly be distinguished from the ability to communicate it. Language study cannot be divorced from language use. However, the editors of this volume point out that language study often is thought of and taught as practice and exercise rather than as a vehicle for living and learning. No wonder so many adolescents find language study in middle schools and high schools boring and inconsequential to their lives.

The contributors in this book illustrate that it does not have to be this way. Rather than learn English in a vacuum, older language learners must experience the power of language in their lives. Therein lies the powerful premise on which this book is based. A central question to keep in mind as you read this book is one that every teacher of English needs to confront: If language cannot be connected to the lives of students, then why study it? You will find this question explored from multiple perspectives throughout the various chapters. The contributors offer practical and powerful insights into language use in the context of reading and language arts classrooms. Kudos to the editors, John Simmons and Lawrence Baines, for compiling thoughtful and thought-provoking chapters that will challenge and reaffirm the beliefs of English language arts teachers.

Richard T. Vacca
Kent State University
Kent, Ohio, USA

CONTRIBUTORS

Michael Angelotti
Professor,
  English Education
College of Education
University of Oklahoma
Norman, Oklahoma, USA

Lawrence Baines
Associate Professor and
  Coordinator of
  Teacher Education
Berry College
Mount Berry, Georgia,
  USA

Pamela Sissi Carroll
Associate Professor and
  Coordinator,
English Education
Florida State University
Tallahassee, Florida, USA

Micah Dial
Proprietor
Evaluation and Data
  Analysis Services, Inc.
Friendswood, Texas, USA

Harold M. Foster
Professor of
  English Education
University of Akron
Akron, Ohio, USA

Anthony Kunkel
English Teacher
Baker County High School
Greater Jacksonville,
  Florida, USA

John S. Mayher
Professor of
  English Education
New York University
New York, New York,
  USA

Kyoko Sato
Professor, Department of
  Secondary Education
California State
  University, Northridge
Northridge, California,
  USA

John S. Simmons
Professor, English
  Education and Reading
Florida State University
Tallahassee, Florida, USA

Walt Wolfram
William C. Friday
  Distinguished Professor
North Carolina State
  University
Raleigh, North Carolina,
  USA

The Context of Language Study in the Contemporary Classroom

JOHN S. SIMMONS AND LAWRENCE BAINES

When I (Baines) first met Desiree, she was sitting at the back of the room in Ms. Jones's third period sophomore English class in a high school in Panama City, Florida, USA. She was shy and I was a stranger, a guest lecturer to her class. My assignment was to present a lesson that would motivate Desiree and the other students in her class to read and write about Arthur Conan Doyle's *The Adventure of the Speckled Band.*

When I asked the class to open their literature texts, Desiree frowned.

"What's wrong?" I asked.

John, a boy slouched deep in his chair, muttered, "She hates to read."

"I don't hate to read," Desiree said. "I like reading. I just hate the words—that's all. Words are just so boring."

"Well, do you like to write?" I asked.

"Writing ain't bad as long as I don't have to write out the sentence. But, really, I guess writing words is just as boring as reading them," Desiree said.

In a way, Desiree's comments represent many students' attitude toward reading and writing in today's society. When cable television and surfing the Internet can transport adolescents instantaneously and graphically into the wide open adult world, sitting at their desks and struggling with words can seem extremely dull.

The U.S. National Assessment of Educational Progress (NAEP) in Writing (Applebee, Langer, Mullis, Latham, & Gentile, 1994) reported that (for persuasive writing), "All students, even at Grade 12, had considerable difficulty moving beyond the minimally developed level...and very few (0 to 3%) wrote elaborated or better responses" (p. 4). The NAEP in Reading (Campbell, Donahue, Reese, & Phillips, 1996) found that only about one third of students achieved at the *Proficient* level and that only "3 to 7% reached the *Advanced* level" (p. xi). The remaining 60% or so of students could perform only at the *Basic* level.

Promoting Experiences with Language

Words are the building blocks of literature and writing, yet many of the movements in educational reform take students outside the linguistic arena, somewhere where words do not matter as much. Although there is much to celebrate about the inclusion of multiculturalism, popular culture, young adult literature, multiple intelligences, the Internet, CD-ROM, and media literacy, these additions may reduce the time students spend studying and manipulating language. Most secondary students still consider language study to mean doing more of the exercises in Warriner's *English Composition and Grammar: Introductory Course* (1988). With an already burgeoning language arts curriculum and the misperception of language study as a mundane subject, it is little wonder that the study of language receives little attention in many middle schools and high schools.

Yet, a student can learn nothing more valuable in school than a mastery over language. Even the chief executives of Fortune 500 companies admit that they consider proficiencies in writing, reading, speaking, and listening to be the most important attributes of a potential employee (Nidds & McGerald, 1995). Although technologies and educational reforms come and go, facility with language is neither fleeting nor fickle. Facility with language is cumulative, integral to thinking, and one gauge by which many people (and testing services) measure intelligence. As much as they have received criticism, the Scholastic Assessment Test, American College Test, Graduate Record Examination, Graduate Management Admission Test, Law School Admission Test, and state high school competency exams still assess a student's verbal ability.

Organization of the Book

The premise of *Language Study in Middle School, High School, and Beyond* is that language should be a central focus for study in the reading and language arts classroom and that gaining mastery over language can be stimulating, enlightening, and enjoyable. This anthology represents a diverse set of viewpoints, each of which describes an approach to language study that is grounded in classroom research and in the context of the emerging trends of the 21st century. In Chapter 1, Simmons describes the evolution of language study in the United States over the past half century. Historically, the curricular and pedagogical approaches to the study of language have been the result of complex interactions among political, sociological, and technological forces.

Chapters 2 through 10 are divided into four strands that contain chapters related to a particular theme. We chose the term "strands" because, despite the apparent variety of approaches to language study offered, we recognized many commonalities among the chapters. The strands themselves were created based on what we perceived to be the needs of secondary teachers of reading and English. Within the strands, each chapter offers practical descriptions of innovative student activities designed to enhance the study of language.

Strand One provides ideas for the teaching of language through literature and the arts. Carroll's Chapter 2 explains ways to approach language study using some recent young adult novels in a transformed middle school environment. In Chapter 3, Angelotti describes a unit he has used in a high school English class that uses aspects of rhythm and blues music and poetry to teach language.

The focus for Strand Two is the interaction that occurs when language study is integrated with the teaching of writing and speaking. In Chapter 4, Kunkel describes some of the drastic measures he had to take in his first year as an English teacher in order to get his students to care about language. Wolfram's Chapter 5 analyzes some of the striking similarities of language use evident in both urban and rural classrooms and offers a convincing rationale for approaching the study of language inductively through oral and written language.

Strand Three is concerned with obstacles to language learning. In Chapter 6, Dial and Baines explain how uncertainty about the meaning of jargon, in this case the jargon of mathematics, can inhibit learning. The authors contend that most misunderstandings in mathematics are not attributable to a confusion over numbers, but to problems of language. Chapter 7 by Sato focuses on the ways that prospective and new teachers attempt to reconcile what they learned about language learning in college with the realities of the classroom. As a teacher educator, Sato has found that many new teachers abandon the research-based practices of language study advocated in the university in favor of an unabashedly teacher-centered, "skill and drill" style once they get a job.

The theme for Strand Four is the future of language study. In Chapter 8, Mayher contends that relating to each student as a human being blessed with talents and faults should be a teacher's top priority. Mayher emphasizes the "human experience of living and learning" as opposed to the current tendency to reduce teachers and students to a set of numbers on a chart. Chapter 9 by Foster describes how any study of language in forthcoming years must be presented within the context of contemporary media, especially film and television. Finally, the text concludes with Chapter 10 by Baines, which discusses some trends that have weakened the status of the written word as the favored mode of communication. Like Foster and other authors represented, Baines believes that language study must embrace technological and sociological change, not run from them.

All of the chapters in this book recommend that the study of language be connected to the lives of students in visceral as well as rational ways. When students recognize that words provide the foundation upon which most learning is based, perhaps the words that Desiree and her classmates find so irrelevant and dull may begin to reverberate with meaning.

References

Applebee, A., Langer, J., Mullis, I., Latham, A., & Gentile, C. (1994). *NAEP 1992 Writing Report Card*. Washington, DC: United States Department of Education, Office of Educational Research and Improvement.

Campbell, J., Donahue, P., Reese, C., & Phillips, G. (1996). *NAEP 1994 Reading Report Card for the Nation and the States*. Washington, DC: United States Department of Education, Office of Educational Research and Improvement.

Nidds, J., & McGerald, J. (1995). Corporate America looks at public education. *Principal, 74*, 22–23.

Warriner, J.E. (1988). English composition and grammar: Introductory course. Orlando, FL: Harcourt Brace Jovanovich.

CHAPTER 1

The Study of Language for Adolescents: A U.S. Historical Perspective

JOHN S. SIMMONS

S uddenly, those of us in the field of English teaching have discerned some stirrings on the topic of language study in the school years beyond the elementary level. *Uncovering the Curriculum* (Strickland & Strickland, 1993) describes a whole language approach to teaching at the secondary level. In 1994, it was followed by Foster's *Crossing Over: Whole Language for Secondary English Teachers*. To those who have been keeping a close eye on English language arts curricula for adolescents and adults, the movement to incorporate language study should come as no surprise. The elements of English teaching that contributed to contemporary language study paradigms have been growing and developing throughout the 20th century. The pace of this growth has accelerated considerably during the past 30 years as new political, social, and cultural influences have made their presence felt in classrooms throughout the United States.

One long-term factor in the evolution of language study has been the slow weakening of the hold that Latinate grammar and prescriptive usage have had on secondary English teachers in the latter half of the 20th century (see Chapter 5 in this volume for further discussion on prescriptive grammar). Armed with solid, consistent research findings that now span over 90 years, teacher educators have continued to apprise English teachers, both preservice and inservice, that formal grammar study has had no positive effect on their students' language capabilities. Most of what teacher educators encountered over the years was resistance to the notion that grammar does not improve reading, writing, or speaking. Moreover, this reluctance to abandon traditional grammar was emphasized by the use of language and writing components in U.S. statewide tests that required knowledge of traditional grammar rules during the 1970s and 1980s. Still, the decreasing presence of once omnipresent grammar series at publishers' exhibits at educational and language arts conventions and on secondary school bookshelves offers unmistakable proof that the study of formal linguistic elements no longer is the primary vehicle for language study in middle schools and high schools.

The loosening of the bonds of prescriptive grammar has contributed significantly to a new movement to teach language. As more teacher educators, supervisors, and classroom practitioners move the focus of language study from the textbook to the utterances and writings of the students, contemporary language products for real purposes have become the teaching strategy in classrooms. When the language examples produced by students replace the rule-related models created by textbook authors and editors, the whole thrust of language study undergoes a conversion from text based to student based.

Still, one must marvel at the resilience and the tenacity of those who teach grammar in the traditional, deductive manner. These teachers have withstood the emergence of structural grammar (remember Roberts's *Patterns of English?*) and the more intense onslaught of Chomskian transformational grammar (remember Roberts's *English series?*) that preoccupied "curriculum innovators" during the 1950s, 1960s, and 1970s. When Warriner's *English Grammar and Composition* series was published in the late 1970s, it must have seemed to many English teachers and teacher educators that prescriptive, Latinate grammar was an immortal, immutable fact of life. Other forces, however, still in their early stages, were beginning to erode the dominance of prescriptive grammar, slowly but inexorably. Prominent among these were "new grammars," sociolinguistic publications, and the emergence of the National Writing Project.

New Directions from an Anglo American Meeting

The impact of student-centered learning on U.S. teaching of English, as articulated by United Kingdom participants at the Anglo American Seminar at Dartmouth College in Hanover, New Hampshire, USA, in August 1966, was not immediate or widespread. In fact, a series of educational reforms and counter-reforms, driven by the ideological shifts of the late 1960s and 1970s, largely diverted attention from the logic and potential value of the student-centered approach. However, through all the turbulent post-Vietnam, post-Watergate years, some voices still could be heard espousing the proposition that it was student language, not textbook language, that should form the basis of the English curriculum. Many Dartmouth participants such as Douglas Barnes, Jimmy Britton, John Dixon, Harold Rosen, and Frank Whitehead articulated this point of view in session after session of the 1966 seminar. In summarizing a major tenet of the U.K. position in his 1967 text *Growth Through English*, Dixon states:

To sum up: language is learnt in operation, not by dummy runs. In English, pupils meet to share their encounters with life, and to do this effectively they move freely between dialogue and monologue—between talk, drama, and writing; and literature, by bringing new voices into the classroom, adds to the store of shared experience. Each pupil takes from the store what he can and what he needs. In so doing he learns to use language to build his own representational world and works to make this fit reality as he experiences it. Problems with the written medium for language raise the need for a different kind of learning. But writing implies a message: the means must be associated with the end, as part of the same lesson. A pupil turns to the teacher he trusts for confirmation of his own doubts and certainties in the validity of what he has said and written; he will also turn to the class, of course, but an adult's experience counts for something. In ordering and composing situations that in some way symbolize life as we know it, we bring order and composure to our inner selves. When a pupil is steeped in language in operation we expect, as he matures, a conceptualizing of his earlier awareness of language, and with this perhaps new insight into himself (as creator of his own world). (p. 13)

The long-range effect of British contributions to the Dartmouth seminar, although muted, has continued to resonate in American pedagogical theory and practice. In addition to the British educators who reaffirmed their students'-language-as-central perspective at every opportunity, U.S. educators such as James Moffett became increasingly vocal in their support of student-centered language learning. One dimension all these scholars emphasized was the need for more oral language activity in secondary classrooms. Before this emphasis was voiced, most language instruction was of the paper and pencil variety. U.S. teachers, often grudgingly, came to the honest admission that, because people talk more than they write and listen more than they read, oral language activity deserved a larger presence in courses of study. Although statewide testing impeded this phase of teaching to some degree, the seed had been planted. The logic of oral language activity and student-centered language instruction became increasingly viable to scores of teacher educators, curriculum supervisors, and classroom teachers.

Student Writing—Problems and Revelations

In the December 8, 1975, issue of *Newsweek* magazine, a feature article appeared titled "Why Johnny Can't Write." Using data from the first National Assessment of Educational Progress test results and from recent declining Scholastic Aptitude Test scores, the authors condemned current practices in writing instruction with U.S. students, especially those in secondary schools. This widely read piece spotlighted what most English educators had known for a long time: relatively little class time was being spent on written composition, and much of what passed for instruction was not effective.

Teachers in the San Francisco Bay area in California, USA, already had begun working on the problem. Starting in 1971, groups gathered each summer to share ideas on writing instruction and to establish a network on how these ideas were working in the classroom throughout the year. When the University of California at Berkeley, more particularly Jim Gray, became involved, the Bay Area Writing Project was born. Soon it gained the support of the National Endowment for the Humanities and became the National Writing Project (NWP). By the summer of 1994, close to 200 Project chapters were providing summer institutes for teachers of all grade levels, kindergarten through college, and across a number of subjects. Through this effort, "writing across the curriculum," which previously had been perceived as another educational cliché, took on substance in countless school districts across the United States.

Several of the major NWP precepts are connected closely to making student-centered language study an integral component of pedagogical philosophy. Among these are the following:

1. Content is of primary importance in the production of written pieces in the classroom.

2. Students must be allowed to express personal feelings, ideas, concerns, and reflections in what they write.

3. Writing needs an audience. Thus, sharing of written products, usually through oral reading, should be an integral part of writing instruction.

4. Sharing is more effectively conducted in small "response" groups (groups of three or four students reading aloud and critiquing one another's work) rather than in all-class oral presentations. These group settings enhance the possibility of peer feedback, still another vital component.

5. The teacher should play the roles of cowriter, positive reinforcer, sympathetic listener, and constructive critiquer rather than the "Giver of the Word" or "Wielder of the Red Pencil."

Soon after the *Newsweek* article, the teaching of writing moved to the forefront of language teachers' consciousness. Educators began to look at Elbow's text *Writing Without Teachers* (1973) a second time. Since then, professional publication about written composition has burgeoned, as a casual glance at the catalogs of virtually all education publishers will reveal. The work of such educators as Sheridan Blau, Donald Graves, Ken MacCrorie, Donald Murray, and Thomas Newkirk has become increasingly influential in classroom teaching activities from kindergarten through college. This work has taken its place beside the contributions of veterans such as James Moffett, Jimmy Britton, Nancy Martin, and John Dixon, all of whom had been urging a movement away from strict formalism in writing instruction for decades. Without exception, this generation of scholars placed strong emphasis on content of writing, value of personal reflection, and sharing of drafts by students.

A significant outgrowth of the widespread attention to the teaching of writing in general, and to the writing process in particular, was the interest in the 1980s in possible connections between reading and writing activity in the classroom. Nancie Atwell was an eighth-grade English teacher in Boothbay Harbor, Maine, USA, when she published her text *In the Middle: Writing, Reading, and Learning with Adolescents* (1987). An immediate success, the book has helped to make collaborative writing an axiom in contemporary English language arts pedagogy. Atwell's description of a workshop strategy through which she led her students to the integration of reading and writing activity represents the substance of her text. The Atwell model was so popular that, within the next 3 years, several new texts appeared that connected reading and writing and the *English Journal* received an extremely large number of submissions from classroom teachers who were trying the collaborative model. Atwell's work clearly inspired another classroom teacher, Linda Rief, to adapt her techniques and combine them with those described by Murray, Graves, and others to create her own observation-based model of collaborative learning. Her book, *Seeking Diversity: Language Arts with Adolescents* (1992), is about as student centered as a methods text can be. Throughout the descriptions of reading-writing connections, it is the students' ideas, perspectives, and concerns that are most important, thus providing another link between contemporary instructional thinking and the evolving paradigm of language study.

Language and Writing in Middle Schools

It is worth noting that at the time their books were published both Atwell and Rief were middle school teachers. Anyone who has been around public schools for any length of time is aware that flexibility of approach usually diminishes among teachers as they ascend through the grades. Elementary school teachers often are the most willing to change, to adapt, or at least to consider innovation. This is the most probable reason that innovative approaches to language study are first incorporated into early-grade curricula. Teachers committed to "language experiences" instructional patterns find the transition to whole language teaching to be relatively easy. As a result, educational publishers have been producing early-grade whole language materials for over a decade. The current battleground of change, however, has been among middle school language arts teachers.

Middle schools, in the early days of their institution, most frequently were curricular replicas of junior high schools. The junior high was a post-World War II phenomenon, created primarily to cope with the burgeoning population of "war babies" that began to finish elementary school in the 1950s. In the late 1960s and throughout the 1970s, as populations grew and racial integration of schools became a reality in the southern U.S. states, the middle school, which typically configured Grades 6, 7, and 8, replaced the junior high school. The initial rationale for this change was housing. In both types of schools the curriculum was a source of conflict, because in junior highs and middle schools, the newly assembled faculties came from the ranks of both elementary schools and high schools. Elementary teachers, usually from upper-elementary grades, basically are student and process centered; high school teachers, on the other hand, are almost without exception connected to content.

The junior highs of the 1940s, 1950s, and 1960s were miniature senior highs in that their programs of study were tilted heavily toward content separation. They featured the four traditional subjects—English, social studies, science, and mathematics—and offered teacher-directed, prescriptive courses. Since that time, however, the middle school has taken a different shape. Current middle school curricular theory features team teaching, collaborative learning, and, above all, student-centered approaches. Teachers who have become familiar with different philosophies of reading-writing connection advocates will recognize that the emerging view of a middle school uses aspects of previously articulated student-centered learning.

Literature and Students' Experience

A new direction in classroom treatment of literature also has had an influence on current thinking about secondary language study. For close to 40 years, college students majoring in English and seeking a secondary school teaching credential left their campuses steeped in critical approaches called "structuralist," "new critical," or "postmodern." Simply stated, the idea was that the teacher or scholar should examine the text from every angle possible (historical, Marxist, Freudian, archetypal) and present the text to the attentive students. These same students then would apply all of this instruction to a reading of the text and draw appropriate conclusions.

Then, in the late 1970s, critics and English educators began rereading Rosenblatt's (1938) *Literature as Exploration*, which proposed that each reader superimposes the totality of his or her own experience on a work of literature during and after reading the text. Thus, the reader and the author become partners in seeking and discovering meaning. In this way, the reader (student) becomes a figure of central importance in the search for meaning. It was not long before a new term was attached to the Rosenblatt revival: reader response. During the early 1980s, Bleich's *Subjective Criticism* and Fish's *Is There a Text in This Class?* offered some extreme variations of the reader response theory. In 1983, however, Probst's *Adolescent Literature* offered a refinement of the Rosenblatt theory relevant to the reading capabilities, needs, and interests of young people. More recently, Andrasick's (1990) *Opening Texts* provides a flexible approach featuring collaborative, interactive strategies meant to enable young readers to escape the constraints of memorized scholarly appraisals and to deal with texts on their own terms and in their own responsive language.

In reader response theories, it is the reader who, as an individual, is the ultimate creator of textual meaning, a meaning that he or she has found through his or her own exploration. Such activities clearly construe literature as being first and foremost a container of experience that becomes more meaningful as it correlates with the life experiences of its readers. Thus, rather than being a dispenser of common culture, the text becomes the preserve of each individual reader. Without experience as a point of departure, readers cannot perceive meaning in texts to their fullest and richest extent.

In this approach, teachers become partners with their students in uncovering and examining meaning. Because such meaning *always* is implied in literary texts, those who use it must necessarily abandon the "one right answer" approach. In turn, this assists both students and teachers in the growing appreciation of connotative meaning in language.

Further Considerations

A few lesser influences on language study also should be noted. One important event was the passage of the "Students' Right to Their Own Language" resolution in 1974 by the National Council of Teachers of English (NCTE). Respect for students' language, especially in oral form, has been promoted by NCTE and its special interest groups ever since. It asks teachers to be at least as aware of students' language as they are of pronouncements in the grammar text, that is, the set of fixed definitions, rules, and usage choices that have dominated traditional language texts for many years.

The multicultural curriculum movement, which has gained momentum in the past 15 years, also has been influential. Much multicultural learning has been conducted as discovery learning, a hallmark of the whole language approach. Project Doublespeak, with its emphasis on the manipulative and obfuscatory tactics used by real speakers with real agendas, has been useful to teachers who urge their students to focus on "real world language." In this NCTE commission, research summaries, scholarly essays, and critiques of public discourse are published to expose the factually inaccurate and frequently hypocritical statements made by politicians and other public figures.

On the other hand, the cultural literacy movements of the past 10 years have openly criticized the movement toward student-centered learning. More intense in their opposition to student-centered language learning are the spokespersons of U.S. groups such as The Christian Coalition, Citizens for Excellence in Education, Concerned Women of America, and Focus on the Family. Often, these groups oppose personal writing, discussion of values, and the use of nonprint media.

Summary

It seems appropriate to reiterate a few basic contentions:

1. Language study is receiving some renewed attention by teachers and scholars.

2. In the past, language and usage often were not taught in ways that enabled students to become engaged learners.

3. How language should be taught is a lengthy conflict.

4. Like all curricular phenomena, contemporary approaches to language study did not arrive suddenly. They have come to us through the inspirational efforts of a number of determined groundbreakers.

The gradual change in thinking about language teaching and learning, discussed in this chapter, has led teachers to a philosophical crossroads. As the scholarly, political, and social factors named earlier influence this philosophical position, teachers of the 21st century will have some basic and significant decisions to make. It is the purpose of the chapters that follow to assist these teachers in making such decisions.

References

Andrasick, K. (1990). *Opening texts*. Portsmouth, NH: Heinemann.

Atwell, N. (1987). *In the middle: Writing, reading, and learning with adolescents*. Portsmouth, NH: Heinemann.

Bleich, D. (1978). *Subjective criticism*. Baltimore, MD: Johns Hopkins University Press.

Dixon, J. (1967). *Growth through English* (3rd ed.). London: Cox & Wyman.

Elbow, P. (1973). *Writing without teachers*. Oxford: Oxford University Press.

Fish, S. (1980). *Is there a text in this class? The authority of interpretive communities*. Cambridge, MA: Harvard University Press.

Foster, H.M. (1994). *Crossing over: Whole language for secondary English teachers*. Fort Worth, TX: Harcourt Brace.

National Council of Teachers of English. (1974, November). *Students' Right to Their Own Language*. Resolution presented at the annual business meeting of the National Council of Teachers of English, New Orleans, LA.

Probst, R. (1983). *Adolescent literature*. Columbus, OH: Merrill.

Rief, L. (1992). *Seeking diversity: Language Arts with adolescents*. Portsmouth, NH: Heinemann.

Roberts, P. (1955). *Patterns of English*. New York: Harcourt Brace.

Rosenblatt, L. (1938). *Literature as exploration*. New York: Appleton Century.

Strickland, K., & Strickland, J. (1993). *Uncovering the curriculum*. Portsmouth, NH: Heinemann.

Warriner, J.E. (1977). *English grammar and composition*. Orlando, FL: Harcourt Brace Jovanovich.

Why Johnny Can't Write. (1975, December 8). *Newsweek*, pp. 58–63.

Strand One

Studying Language
Through Literature
and the Arts

CHAPTER 2

A (W)Hole in the Middle: Language Study for Transformed Middle Schools

PAMELA SISSI CARROLL

Among the many mistakes I made as a teacher of middle school English language arts courses when I began teaching at that level in 1981, the following 10 have come back to haunt me. I am reminded of these mistakes when I see other beginning teachers struggle to preserve order in a classroom; I am reminded of them whenever I see teachers whose years of experience have insulated them against the need to engage in critical self-evaluation of their teaching and honest assessment of their students' learning. I would like to apologize to my former students because of the following:

1. I equated a quiet classroom with a good classroom, and I thought that students who could not avoid talking with their friends were immature and rude.

2. I expected all students to use the same processes to learn course material, and to learn it at a pace

that was synchronized with the pace of the rest of the class.

3. I expected all students to be eager to learn the lessons that I had planned every day. Although I was aware that the other (and the most important) parts of their worlds existed outside of my classroom, I often could not find ways to bring together the worlds beyond and within my classroom.

4. On more than one occasion, I indignantly asked a room filled with 12-year-olds, "Why don't you act like adults?" just because many of them had begun to look like adults.

5. I embarrassed some students by bragging about the quality of their compositions in front of their peers, unaware that the codes of some peer groups forbade its members from doing well in school.

6. I could do nothing to alleviate the embarrassment of students who, in their excitement to contribute to a class discussion, raised their hands and shouted, "Mom!"

7. I taught grammar lessons in a contextual vacuum and dodged the biggest question a teacher must ask after each lesson, "So what?" because I knew I would be left without an answer.

8. I asked students to write and even gave them a head start by supplying topics, forms, length requirements, and deadlines, but I never talked with them about how to generate ideas, how to use writing as thinking, or how to assess the effectiveness of their written compositions.

9. I told students about authors and about literature, but I failed to get out of their way long enough to let them experience literature.

10. I had no idea how to help the first Vietnamese student who arrived in my class with a frightened glance and very little English, or the first hearing-disabled student who came to the class in tears because she hated being followed from class to class by an interpreter, or the gregarious boy in a wheelchair who needed twice as long as everyone else to complete his assignments because of damage to his nervous system.

When I reflect on the problems that prompted this list of apologies, I realize that the problems have one thing in common: when I began teaching English language arts at the middle school level, I believed that my job was to teach the *subject* of English. What I have learned since is that my job is to teach *students*. I have learned that student-centered instructional approaches allow teachers to take advantage of students' innate talents and tendencies as language users.

Student-Centered Language Study for Today's Transformed Middle Schools

Unlike the teacher-centered approach that I had tried for several years, student-centered approaches are appropriate in the atmosphere of today's transformed middle schools in the United States. They allow for classrooms that are filled with the noise of collaborative inquiry; they allow for attention to individual learning styles; they encourage the use of language for meaningful purposes; and they give attention to the physical, psychosocial, and intellectual characteristics of young adolescents.

In 1989, the Carnegie Council on Adolescent Development published its benchmark report, *Turning Points: Preparing American Youth for the 21st Century*. The report cited disturbing realities regarding the lack of academic development among young Americans, and addressed the growing number of social, environmental, moral, and economic factors that continually put adolescents in jeopardy of failing to become productive adult members of society. The report called for schools to be transformed in the following ways:

1. Large schools should be divided into smaller communities (teams) for learning.

2. A common core of knowledge should be presented to all students, regardless of the learning ability levels they demonstrate; thus, ability-group tracking should be eliminated.

3. Scheduling and team-teaching organization should promote success of all students.

4. Teachers and principals should have the primary responsibility and obligation to effect changes within the school.

5. Teachers should be prepared specifically to teach at the middle grades level.

6. Good health should be a focal issue for all students, teachers, and staff.

7. Alliances among teachers, administrators, and students' families should be fostered.

8. Alliances with community-based businesses and organizations should be developed. (p. 36)

The kind of transformed school that is promoted in *Turning Points* is an environment in which student-centered approaches can thrive. On the following page are examples how teacher and student roles are expanded in a transformed middle school.

- As members of interdisciplinary teams of teachers of a small community of learners (usually situations in which four academic-area teachers have the same 150 or so students), language arts teachers are able to work across the curriculum to suggest, plan, and implement the kind of authentic language-using and language-learning experiences that are characteristic of student-centered approaches.

- In middle schools where ability-group tracking is eliminated, the collaborative learning opportunities that characterize student-centered classes provide all students with opportunities to succeed.

- In middle schools where teachers are empowered to make decisions on behalf of their students, they are not bound by tradition or by others' expectations to teach aspects of language, such as grammar and mechanics, in fragmented and isolated ways.

Transformed middle schools are receptive sites for language-rich instructional strategies and for the dynamic curricula and class activities in which student-centered approaches are adopted.

Why Student-Centered Approaches Are Developmentally Appropriate for Today's Young Adolescents

Today's teachers of middle school students recognize that the physical, psychosocial, and intellectual characteristics of young adolescents (ages 10–14) set those students apart from the children of elementary schools and the teens of high schools. Many teachers of English language arts now realize that young adolescents' needs in each of these areas can be addressed and met in classes that are grounded in student-centered approaches; it may be in their English language arts courses that students first articulate and grapple with the most formidable question of adolescence: "Who am I?"

Physical characteristics of young adolescents include growth spurts for females between the ages of 10 and 14, and growth spurts for males between the ages of 12 and 16. Twelve is the average age for the beginning of obvious changes in girls' body shapes and for menarche; 14 is the average age when males manifest obvious signs of physical maturation, such as the appearance of body hair, muscle definition, and arms, noses, and ears that temporarily are out of proportion with the rest of the body. When the females in a seventh-grade class are physically more mature than males, predictable problems arise. Some females are embarrassed into withdrawal by the attention they receive from males because of their maturing bodies; some are jealous because their friends have developed before them and are getting all of the boys' attention; others become obsessed with their appearance to the point of engaging in dangerous behaviors such as self-starvation and purging. Males who develop physically before their peers are treated as class leaders and are expected to act more like adults than their less physically mature classmates.

Biological changes such as metabolic and hormonal fluctuation also occur in young adolescents of both genders. These changes account for students' erratic shifts among listlessness, restlessness, and enthusiasm; they also account for the ravenous and bizarre appetites of many young teens, and for acne on some students' bodies. Hormonal changes also produce females who feel happy with themselves one day and disgusted with themselves the next, and males who are preoccupied by hints of sexuality in those around them and in the media. These and other physical changes often produce confusion and dismay for young adolescents; those who previously had been acquainted with their own bodies find themselves with bodies they neither feel comfortable with nor recognize as their own. Physical changes have a lasting impact on young adolescents' psychosocial characteristics, and thus can be traced as a cause of the kind of behavior middle school students exhibit in school.

The Student-Centered Classroom

As they seek to understand their changing bodies, young adolescents also seek to understand themselves as psychological and social creatures. They raise and explore questions about their sexuality, their changing relationships with family members and peers, and their own personalities. As young teens become more and more dependent on identification with a peer group, a tension grows between their sense of loyalty to their families and old friends and allegiance to a new group. Their moods frequently fluctuate; one day a female adolescent may want to play with a doll and be babied by her teachers, and the next day she may expect her teachers to treat her as an adult. Similarly, a male may look forward to playing in his fort in the woods one afternoon, only to spend the next afternoon practicing talking to girls on the telephone. In student-centered classrooms, teachers can situate the question "Who am I?" as an underlying theme for units of study in which literature, composition, speaking, media, and metacognitive thinking activities are integrated. Foster (1994) explains that, in student-centered classrooms, young teenagers are given the freedom and an impetus to do the following:

- search for themselves, seeking answers to problems and issues that perplex them through reading, writing, seeing, and listening experiences that make sense to them;

- use language to communicate thoughts and feelings that are important for them to express;

- debate and ponder issues important to the community as well as the individual;

- grow as language users, becoming strong readers, writers, listeners, and viewers; and
- empathize with the different ways groups use language and grow to understand how audiences and situations shape the nature of the language. (p. 12)

Teachers who draw on student-centered approaches to language study believe that the physical and psychological environment of a classroom must be conducive to language use and language learning. In describing settings that support student-centered teaching and learning, Noden and Vacca (1994) suggest arranging the furniture in English classrooms into small groupings that "invite reading, speaking, discussing, publishing, thinking, sharing, and dramatizing... an environment that welcomes students as active participants rather than pigeonholes them as passive recipients" (p. 22). Unlike traditional classrooms in which desks and chairs are arranged in rows and students are expected to stay quietly in their seats for entire class periods, this kind of configuration will encourage students to move around the room. The configuration thus gives students opportunities to stretch their growing bodies, to release some of their physical energy, to occasionally satisfy urges to socialize, or to withdraw into isolation when they feel the need to be alone.

In addition to providing a productive physical environment, English language arts teachers who incorporate student-centered approaches are careful to provide middle school students with a low-risk psychological environment in which adolescents can experiment with their newly emerging personalities, values systems, and understandings. Although the advisor-advisee arrangement that is incorporated in many middle schools provides a pairing of small groups of students with a trusted adult on a daily basis, it is often the English language arts teacher to whom students turn for encouragement and advice because these teachers emphasize the human element in their instruction. The following academic activities encourage students to explore questions about their own identities, and also nudge them beyond egocentrism to a broader, more socially aware perspective:

- preparing a written, illustrated report after conducting research and taking photographs of places in the community that are significant for the student;

- planning and recording interviews with adults in a community-based oral history project;

- reading and responding to stories by and about people from cultures similar to—and different from—the students' own;

- seeking and synthesizing information about the habits and attitudes of teens from across the world using the Internet;

- writing and illustrating fables and other stories to present to elementary school students during story time;

- watching television advertisements and evaluating them critically in terms of the messages they intend to send viewers; and

- critically evaluating movies in terms of the hidden messages they send to adolescents about violence, love, or family loyalty.

Teachers with student-centered stances also are able to address the differences in intellectual development that occur during middle school years. Young adolescents usually begin to show signs of developing the capacity to think abstractly. Characteristics of this more advanced stage of thinking include the ability to engage in contrary-to-fact reasoning, to use a second symbol system such as algebra and metaphors, and to practice hypothetical-deductive reasoning. These and other changes in intellectual capacity increase the opportunities for young adolescents to enjoy puns and satire, to experiment with figurative language, and to consider many possible solutions to problems.

In student-centered classrooms, students are challenged to learn to *think*, not merely to learn to *remember* information. For example, a teacher who is a proponent of student-centered practices does not insist that students memorize what she believes to be "the meaning" of the title of Robert Frost's poem "Nothing Gold Can Stay." Instead, the teacher encourages students to use reading response journals and class discussion to construct their own meanings for the title, requiring only that students consider the title within the context of the poem itself. Discussion of the poem then involves an exploration of different students' readings and interpretations; the teacher is involved in meaning making with students but is not responsible for transmitting information to them.

In classrooms like this one, students also are treated as writers who have real purposes for writing. Instead of composing an essay that is read only by the teacher, for example, an eighth grader might write a letter to a group of fifth graders about what they can expect in middle school. A seventh grader might write to the city parks association requesting information about the recreational soccer program for adolescent females. A sixth grader might write a narrative about his fishing trip with his grandfather, with the intention of giving the story to his grandfather at his 60th birthday party. Each of these writing activities is based on the student writer's desire to communicate an idea to a real audience that is important for him or her. None of these writing activities serves merely to produce a sample of composition that a teacher can read and evaluate. The effectiveness of the compositions will be determined by readers' responses and reactions, rather than writing solely for a grade. Teachers who encourage students to engage in these kinds of activities are helping them connect new learning with their previous experiences and knowledge. It is at the intersection of new and past understandings that learning occurs. Intellectual development happens as a consequence of minds being engaged in the kind of authentic meaning-making activities that is characteristic of the student-centered orientation.

The Language Arts Curriculum in Middle Schools: Young Adult Literature and Student-Centered Approaches

Teachers who have an orientation toward student-centered approaches are likely to be familiar with young adult literature and its potential as a curricular staple in middle school language arts classrooms—and in social studies, science, mathematics, art, music, physical education, and other classes at the middle level. Teachers who are interested in making a gradual shift toward a student-centered orientation may wish to become more familiar with young adult fiction and nonfiction. As they read young adult books, teachers are likely to discover that young adult literature is particularly appropriate for middle school readers for several reasons, including the following:

- The protagonists in young adult literature are most often teenagers themselves; middle school readers are attracted to stories that feature characters who are their age and to characters who speak their language.

- Problems that characters experience in young adult novels often mirror problems that many adolescents experience, such as alienation, conflicts with parents, changing relationships with peers, pressure to do well in school and other activities, and girl-friend or boyfriend disputes.

- In many young adult books, characters are placed in extreme situations, such as losing parents in a car crash, dealing with a friend's realization that he or she is homosexual, discovering that a sibling has a drug problem or a terminal disease, or living through a shipwreck only to awaken blind and almost completely alone. Middle school readers are curious about how other young people would respond to these extreme situations, yet they enjoy the comfortable distance from the problems that literature provides.

- Many popular young adult books present factual information for teen readers who are interested in learning about health issues, historical events, famous athletes, popular entertainers, important scientists, and well-known writers.

- Young adult books typically are shorter and move more quickly than the books that older teens and adults choose to read, with less attention to descriptive details than is typical of adult literature.

- When teams of teachers include it in interdisciplinary thematic units, young adult literature can enhance instruction across the curriculum.

In the following section, I will present activities that are appropriate for student readers in middle school language arts classes, and that are consistent with a student-centered orientation. The activities I describe are for whole-class and small-group activities associated with the young adult book *Freak the Mighty*, by Rodman Philbrick (1993); however, the framework in which teaching and learning activities are presented may help teachers conceptualize a scheme for organizing literature-based thematic units around almost any book. This frame may be especially helpful for teachers who are

beginning to move toward a student-centered orientation because it provides an uncomplicated structure for listing activities in which language skills are integrated. It also has a section where tie-ins for interdisciplinary teaming and for
technological enhancement are suggested. I encourage teachers to modify and transfer the activities to the young adult
books that are favorites among their own students.

Teaching *Freak the Mighty* in a Student-Centered Classroom

Freak the Mighty is a delightful and poignant book
about Kevin, or "Freak," a young boy whose body never grows
but whose brain cannot stop growing, and Max, or "Mighty,"
a boy whose body seems to never stop growing but whose intelligence has developed slowly. This odd pair, who together
become "Freak the Mighty," are inseparable friends. To make
their traveling around school and the neighborhood easier,
Kevin rides everywhere on top of Max's shoulders; from this
position, he not only navigates, but he also teaches Max his
own vocabulary words (which are defined in the novel's glossary) and hard-to-believe stories. The two characters have a
series of exciting and dangerous adventures. When Max's
father gets out of jail and kidnaps his son, Kevin outsmarts
Max's father and becomes a hero. Soon, though, Kevin's physical condition grows critical. Although Kevin had convinced
Max that doctors were going to turn him into the world's first
human robot, his body finally quits. Kevin leaves Max—and
others whose lives he touches—a legacy of strength, humor,
and confidence.

Teaching and Learning Activities: Suggestions for a Whole-Class Reading of *Freak the Mighty*

1. A "new and improved" ending. In one of the closing
episodes of the book, Kevin's mother, "the Fair Gwen," hosts

a 13th birthday party for her son. It is during the party that Kevin has a seizure and must be taken to the hospital, where he dies a few days later. Until this point, some readers may have been convinced, as was Max, that Kevin's condition would be changed by an operation, one that Kevin claimed would make him the world's first human robot. Ask the class to rewrite the end of the book, imagining that Kevin has the operation and receives robotic parts. The new endings should add an adventure that is consistent with the novel, in terms of setting, characters, language, and tone. One example to offer students is the addition of an episode in which Max and the "new and improved" robotic Kevin again face "Killer Kane," Max's criminal father. Another possible ending would be an episode in which Kevin uses his new body along with his new computer to become the academic and athletic hero of his junior high school, with Max as his advisor. Some may wish to dramatize and videotape their episode additions to show to the class. This activity would allow those readers who are uncomfortable with the fact that Kevin dies in the book to provide classmates with a humorous or suspenseful alternative, yet it also encourages them to pay close attention to the original text when trying to adhere to the settings, characters, language, and tone of the novel.

2. Disabilities: Facts and fiction. After students have read the 160-page novel, many will have questions about the physical condition from which Kevin suffered, and about other disabilities. Their curiosity may provide a good opportunity to invite a guest or panel of guest speakers to talk with middle school students about various physical and mental disabilities. The guests might be a blend of health-care professionals and people with disabilities who are eager to help others understand their problems and the ways in which those with disabilities also are like those without disabilities. Students should prepare for guest visits by conducting research about the particular disabilities the speakers will address, then using the research notes to write specific questions that they wish to ask. Library resources, CD-ROM encyclopedia disks, and various World Wide Web sites could be used as research resources. Teachers may wish to contact local health-care organizations and social services for information about appropriate sources of information for student research and for the names of possible speakers.

Following the guest speaker presentation, students might work in collaborative groups to create either a factual report or a fictitious but fact-based story about a day in the life of a disabled person. A related activity would have students reading biographies of famous people with disabilities; a biography of famous contemporary physicist and philosopher Stephen Hawking certainly would appeal to Kevin and the middle school readers who share the character's enthusiasm for science.

Students also would be likely to benefit from conducting similar research regarding the programs designed to meet the needs of students with disabilities that are in place in their school system. The culminating step of this project, instead of composing a written report or an article, could be an oral presentation of the information during a meeting of the school's Parent-Teacher Organization or to students in one or more of the elementary schools that are in the neighborhood of the middle school. The increased awareness and understanding that results from these community and school-based research projects have the potential to help students learn to seek ways in which life is mirrored in literature and to appreciate differences; the projects may even lead toward interest in volunteering in programs that serve people with special needs.

3. Glossary creation. In an activity that will encourage students to make personal connections with literature, they could be required to create a glossary, much like "Freak's Dictionary" on pages 161–169 of the book, in which they identify, define, and create an illustration for the terms that they use in unique ways. Students might prepare the glossary for the benefit of a hopelessly out-of-touch teacher, a parent, or even a younger sibling. Each could select a few entries to share orally with the class; then the class could work together to compile and publish its own glossary and title it something like "On Our Own Terms." It will be important that students study "Freak's Dictionary" and discuss its style and the kinds of words that are included before they begin collecting words for their own glossaries. This project could be introduced when students first begin reading the novel and could continue, with a minimum number of entries required each week, until the study of the novel and the unit in which it is included is completed. This activity, which lends itself either to individual or small-group work, gives students an impetus for answering the question "Who am I?" in terms of the language they use.

Integrated Language Activities Checklist

Speaking

- Students read aloud or dramatize their original, additional episodes in which Kevin has a robotic body.
- Students interview guest speakers about people with disabilities or talk to representatives from the school system's various programs for students with special needs.
- Students orally present their reports or stories about those with disabilities to classmates or to younger students.

- Students give oral presentations of personal glossary terms, modeled after "Freak's Dictionary," to the class.

Listening

- Students listen as audience members when classmates read or dramatize an added episode.

- Students listen as they interview guest speaker(s); they are audience members who must listen closely in order to ask pertinent questions of the speaker.

- Students listen to questions of classmates as they present glossary terms, and listen as audience members suggest classmates' best terms—those that should be included in the class glossary.

Reading

- Students read the novel individually and silently or aloud as a class.

- Students read research information about disabilities in order to prepare for a guest speaker interview.

- Students may read a biography, such as one of Stephen Hawking.

- Students read and serve as editors for others' reports and stories or episode additions.

- Students read "Freak's Dictionary" with an eye for the style of the entries, and they read their own and classmates' glossary terms in order to suggest entries for the class glossary.

Writing

- Students write additional episodes, using the author's style as a model.

- Students write reports or stories based on facts they compile by taking notes from various resources.

- Students write their own individual and class glossary.
- Students may be asked to write evaluative comments when classmates give oral presentations related to the book.

Suggestions for Interdisciplinary Tie-Ins and Technology Enhancement

Science. Lessons or assignments might focus on degenerative diseases or on the current state of robotics.

Mathematics. Lessons might focus on proportions, weights, and measurements, using problems related to the differences in Kevin's and Max's height, weight, and need for calories.

Social Studies. Lessons might lead toward a survey of the services provided to people with disabilities in the area; they might focus on legal issues concerning people with disabilities, including parking privileges and discrimination.

Technology. Teachers and students might use computers and the Internet to conduct research and to gather information for the reports related to the study of the novel; use CD-ROM encyclopedia disks as reference resources; have students videotape their stories and oral report presentations; or have students use word processors to prepare their reports and stories.

Evaluation Options

The English language arts teacher may choose to evaluate students' performance as language users in any of the integrated activities mentioned in the previous sections of this chapter. Some teachers will choose, because of personal preference or school policies, to evaluate students' progress on language activities throughout the study of the novel; those teachers will collect, grade, and return written reports and stories, and will grade oral presentations and performances in the order that the products are completed. They will be likely to do their grading alone, without consultation with other teachers from the other subject areas, even if all of the teachers have agreed to teach an interdisciplinary thematic unit in which the novel is a central feature.

The following suggestions are offered, however, for teachers who are able and willing to take one step away from traditional assessment toward more integrated processes. When possible, students should be required to prepare a portfolio of the work related to the novel and to the thematically related activities in which they engage across the curriculum. The portfolio is a particularly promising assessment alternative when the English language arts teacher is working as a member of a team that has centered an interdisciplinary thematic unit around study of a novel.

The portfolio will start as a folder, preferably an accordion-pleated one, in which students keep all notes, drafts, questions, products, and formative evaluative comments—self-evaluation checklists, evaluations given by peers during peer editing and response time, and those given when peers are audience members for oral presentations—associated with the interdisciplinary concentration or thematic units in which a novel is the central feature.

The student may be instructed, at the completion of the study of the novel or of the thematic unit, to prepare the portfolio for submission to the interdisciplinary team of teachers who collaborated to implement the unit of study. In order to prepare the portfolio, students should be given instructions about the number and nature of artifacts to include. For each artifact (essay, letter, report, or self-evaluative checklist) the student may write a short cover statement explaining what the artifact demonstrates in terms of his or her growth as a thinker. In addition, students may write a full cover letter to the team of teachers, explaining their responses to the unit as a whole. These portfolio activities will encourage students to engage in metacognitive and critical thinking. The evaluation itself is an opportunity for purposeful use of language for learning.

Conclusion

English language arts classrooms in today's transformed middle schools are places where students can be welcomed as language users and language learners. Interdisciplinary teams of teachers work together to help students make connections within and between subjects, and to help them use language for meaningful purposes. In classes in which student-centered approaches are implemented in lessons like those described in this chapter, the artificial distinction between "school world" and "real world" is eliminated because students are using language to explore questions about themselves and their world.

Student-centered approaches to teaching language offer little to teachers who feel compelled to present themselves as the single authority in their classrooms, who insist that students remain quiet and still during instruction regardless of their learning styles, and who ignore that students have lives that extend beyond the classroom. Student-centered approaches also offer little for teachers who choose to believe that teaching to the middle ability range is the best that teachers can be expected to do. In other words, a student-centered approach to language study would not have worked for the teacher I was several years ago, a teacher who valued subject matter over the students who studied it.

Given the realities of a school's culture and resources, of class sizes and standardized testing, I found that my own deliberate move toward student-centered instruction would have to be gradual. I suspect that many teachers are in a similar situation today. Yet I urge teachers at the middle school level to begin taking steps toward instruction that focuses on students as active language users and learners. The first step may be for us teachers to ask ourselves what we are willing to do in order to help students learn to use language in ways that will help them understand and navigate adolescence, and that eventually will carry them into adulthood.

References

Carnegie Council on Adolescent Development. (1989). *Turning points: Preparing American youth for the 21st century.* New York: Carnegie Corporation.

Foster, H.M. (1994). *Crossing over: Whole language for secondary English teachers.* Forth Worth, TX: Harcourt Brace.

Noden, H.R., & Vacca, R.T. (1994). *Whole language in middle and secondary classrooms.* New York: HarperCollins.

Children's Literature Reference

Philbrick, R. (1993). *Freak the mighty.* New York: Scholastic.

CHAPTER 3

Poetics, Poetry Reading, and Poetry Writing

MICHAEL ANGELOTTI

While supervising a student teaching intern not long ago, I discovered a student anthology of blues lyrics on the cooperating teacher's desk. I flipped the pages as its ninth-grade authors made their way to their tables in the classroom; I read poems and noticed forms. The students wrote blues lyrics that connected to their lives. They derived form and invented content from what they heard in the music and saw in the lyric. They demonstrated an internalized sense of poetics developed over a lifetime. Among the other elements of writing a poem, the following student examples indicate that they experimented with visual effects and presentation; rhythm, rhyme, and repetition; and line breaks and humor:

I got the blues...I got the
Sunday night homework blues....

Should have done it on Friday,
don't know what to say.
I guess I forgot,

and now I'll have to pay.

I got the blues...I got the
Sunday night homework blues....

from *Sunday Night Homework Blues*
(Anonymous)

The students also made use of figurative language, as shown in the following poem:

I got the blues, my heart's in the can
I got the blues, my heart's in the can
My heart's in the can, I ain't got no man
I got the blues

from *Bad Man Blues*
by Kathleen Gardenhire

The language arts and social studies teachers team taught this group of ninth-grade students through the year. They began the fall term with a multicultural awareness unit that included a study of the blues, and within that cluster of activities, blues music. The teachers wanted to set the tone for the school year by beginning with an interesting unit close to the personal experiences of their students.

Blues Lyrics and the Study of Poetics

As a relatively uncomplicated form of poetry, blues lyrics offer excellent beginning material for a study of poetics. When written and read, they look like poems, sound like poems, and feel like poems. They are rhythmic, often use rhyme, alliteration, and metaphor, and are written in lines. Students practice expressive language, line breaks, word choice, the music of language in verse, figurative language, exaggeration, and humor. They discover a simple medium for putting emotion, trouble, and joy to print and they notice the poetry in everyday life. Students can engage the blues lyric because in combination with the music, its content is interesting, its language is readable, and its form is uncomplicated. They are able to comprehend the art and text of a blues song in a relatively short time. Students readily compose meanings, compose text, and achieve success with this kind of literature both in reading and in writing, although, as is the case with most adult literature, how deeply the experience embedded in blues music resonates for students of this age is questionable. However, they will connect to some degree because they feel deeply about their own lives.

One approach, essentially followed in this class, had students listen to a sampling of blues songs provided by the teacher or other students while examining the lyrics on overhead transparencies. In small groups, the class would explore blues lyrics as poetry and as expressions of culture, connect the blues form to their personal histories, and write blues poems individually and in collaboration. They then would share the poems as individual readings, small-group choral readings, or individual and group songs, with and without guitar or other musical accompaniment. Transparencies of student blues poems would motivate final editing and enhance their presentations. To explore possibilities for visual presentation of their poems, students also would prepare their pieces during computer lab time, with the teacher's assistance. In the end, students selected from their own work for the class anthology.

Clearly, many positive things in this classroom advanced student understandings of poetry and encouraged language development. The students worked with material they could and wanted to access experientially and linguistically, and the classroom culture allowed them to engage content and processes at developmental levels in which they could function comfortably. The teacher, sensitive to the classroom community, led her students through a carefully developed sequence of experiences and remained cognizant of the specific content objectives and appropriate learning processes for her students. They learned something of poetics as it exists in the blues form and of poetry in general. They practiced language and social interaction, and, likely, felt good about some success they achieved.

Found Poems and the Study of Poetics

Another strategy the English teacher used was to engage her students in Found Poem activities, an approach that can effectively enhance understandings of poetics by middle school and high school students. It integrates the study of prose forms such as the novel and the use of "found" poems. Dunning and Stafford (1992, pp. 3–4) describe Found Poetry as "interesting, ordinary prose," not intentionally poetic or "artistically arranged" as are poetry, song lyrics, or advertising. As examples of possible Found Poem sources, the authors suggest that "you can find moving, rich language in books, on walls, even in junk mail." They also identify conversations, television shows, radio, newspapers, bulletin boards, menus, and notes left on desks as possible sources. The found content is "raw material" to be used by the Found Poet.

Found Poetry activities allow the student to apply knowledge of poetics to prose material to discover potentially rich poetic material, then recompose the material into poems. The student is relieved of the pressure of inventing content while concentrating on composing the final piece. Although it could be argued that the activities involved essentially are rearranging or revising text, the meaning of the prose text belongs to the reader who, as a writer, must structure the meaning into a new literary form. It is likely that each Found Poet reading the same prose text would compose somewhat different meanings and poetic versions than those of any other writer. In addition, the context of the poem has changed from the world of the book to the world of the Found Poet. In a very real sense, practice in composing and applying poetic knowledge is inherent in the Found Poem activity. As a result of productive Found Poem activities, students may become more focused readers of prose and become more conscientious writers of poetry.

One of the activities following the blues mini-unit in the ninth-grade curriculum guide was a literary study of Ray Bradbury's *Fahrenheit 451* as part of a "constitutional rights" thematic unit. The teachers decided that a Found Poem approach would allow them to engage their students in a close reading of the novel while allowing for personal involvement and response. It also would encourage students to compose literary writing. One product of this approach was a second student anthology: *451 Found Poems*. The strategy was simple. After preliminary work establishing concepts related to the notion of Found Poems, students would seek language in their readings of *Fahrenheit 451* that appeared poetic. Mainly, they were drawing on an internalized sense of poetics, their own concepts of what makes a poem, applying that to prose, imagining the possible poem, then selecting from the possibilities those that stood the best chance of making interesting poems after treatment by the Found Poet. Treatment included deciding how much of the prose text to omit, shaping the poem, deciding line breaks, and deleting and adding words and punctuation. Two examples from the classroom activity follow, for which I invite the reader to imagine the application of poetics.

The War

The war began and ended in that instant.
Later, the men could not say if they had really seen anything.

Perhaps the merest flourish of light and motion in the sky.
Perhaps the bombs were there,

the jets,
ten miles,
five miles,
one mile,
Up for the merest instant, like grain thrown over by a great
sowing hand.
The bombs drifting with dreadful swiftness,
yet sudden,
slowness,
down upon the morning city,
they had left.

The bombardment was to all intents and purposes finished,
the jets had
sighted their target.
The war had begun and ended in that instant.

Finder: Nick Sanders
From: *Fahrenheit 451*, p. 158
Author: Ray Bradbury

a man and a woman

he saw himself in her eyes
suspended in two shiny drops of water
himself dark and tiny in fine detail

the lines about his mouth
everything there
as if her eyes were two miraculous
bits of violet amber that might
capture and hold him intact

Finder: Stephanie Hayes
From: *Fahrenheit 451*, p. 7
Author: Ray Bradbury

The collection of Found Poems was uniformly excellent. The notion of Found Poems, of course, is not new, although its potential in today's classrooms is largely untapped

by many teachers. We should rethink its applications, particularly in regard to teaching poetry. The following are my final observations on the blues and Found Poetry approaches to teaching poetics as described to this point:

- Blues lyrics were treated much like Found Poems.

- Continuing the Found Poems strategy from one unit to the next served to connect understandings and applications of one learning context to another, reinforcing language processing strategies as well as understandings of poetics and literary form.

- The Found Poems were, from an adult perspective, significantly richer poems than the blues poems.

- My initial sense was that either activity could precede and positively influence student performance in the other.

- Now I wonder if introducing the Found Poem activity first would result in better blues poems.

Beyond the Blues and Found Poems

Students would seem at this point to be grounded enough in poetics and in reading and writing poetry to engage modern, then classic poems; that is, they should begin with the more familiar language, form, and content of contemporary poetry, including blues and other popular poetic expression, and move backward in time to the more unfamiliar language, form, and content of more traditionally anthologized works. Strategically the key points to consider are accessibility of language, identification with content, and experience with transacting form. Students must be able to respond at an independent reading level. The movement should be deliberate, but not necessarily linear. For example, once the initial work with poetics is done, content becomes increasingly more important than form for independent reading and response. Students have acquired enough of a grounding in poetics and form to get to the essential content. A mix of modern and classic as part of a thematic unit or series of thematic units can be effective: William Carlos Williams, Edgar Allan Poe, William Stafford, a Shakespearean sonnet or a segment from *Macbeth*, or Milton's *Paradise Lost*. Continued use of Found Poem approaches adapted to the varieties of prose forms can serve to deepen understandings of both the prose and poetry forms. The keys to working developmentally, especially in regard to classical forms, are incremental learning and finding the most appropriate place for students to begin. Teachers can begin with small chunks of text and work to longer pieces over time and academic years. Found Poems are an effective starting point for most groups to introduce basic poetics. For the ninth graders of this discussion, the blues were personally relevant. *Fahrenheit 451* also was effective, with the blues understandings and practice as a comfortable transition. For other groups, pop music, newspaper headlines, advertisements, or cereal box print may work better as beginning material. However, my guess is that the blues and Found Poems are universal enough to adapt to most learners, in and out of school.

Poetics and Seventh Graders

Later in that school year, working with a group of seventh graders as a poet-in-residence at a rural Oklahoma middle school, I introduced them to a favorite poem of mine: "Bullfrogs" by David Allan Evans. It is a poem that has never failed me, no matter the audience: children, college seniors, or senior citizens. I often refer to it as a perfect teaching poem. It works mainly because its language, subject matter, and form are accessible to almost every reader, regardless of personal history. Most importantly, it is a very good poem. The complete poem is written as follows:

Bullfrogs

- for Ernie, Larry, and Bob

sipping a Schlitz
we cut off the legs,
packed them in ice, then
shucked the rest back into
the pond for turtles

ready to go home
we looked down and saw
what we had thrown back in:
quiet-bulging eyes nudging along
the moss's edge, looking up at us,

asking for their legs.

—David Allan Evans
Poem originally published in *oakwood*
Used by permission of author.

On this day, I presented a green transparency of the poem on an overhead projector, blocking the title and last line. My first strategy was to create a setting that would encourage the students to engage the content and respond independently to the poem itself. Titles can be quite directive and often tell in advance the subject of the poem; such is the case with "Bullfrogs." I omitted the title on the transparency to spark curiosity and to induce a problem-solving attitude that could lead students to their own internal questioning: "Schlitz? What's that? Cut off the legs? Of what? Who? What is 'shucked'? Oh, must mean tossed. Into the pond for turtles? Is this about hunting frogs? What is this piece of writing about?" At the same time, reading the body of the poem would invoke a network of images, meanings, and responses for the students, connecting their personal experiences to the language, content, and form of the poem.

I blocked the last line because of its dramatic impact, a topic I would address with the class later, and because the last line visible to them initially, "the moss's edge, looking up at us," conveys a sense of closure that can deceive the reader momentarily into thinking the poem has ended. This intensifies the surprise and dramatic impact of the actual last line: "asking for their legs." I wanted to focus on the function of surprise in poetry and on the importance of interpretive reading, oral and subvocal, not only to enhance the enjoyment of poetry reading, but also to promote effective revision strategies in poetry writing. During the class session I would model interpretive reading of this poem, with some illustration of dramatic excess, hopefully humorous. I also would allow and encourage the students to practice interpretive reading of both their own texts and those written by others, a highly useful skill that I have observed to be largely neglected in the schools I have visited.

Providing the visual presentation of the poem using an overhead projector is crucial to whole-class work because the lighted visual (especially on a green transparency) encourages focus on the learning prompt. The piece becomes inescapably large for student reading, and the instructor is able to isolate and block parts of the poem to discuss poetics. Incidental and independent learning of poetics by individual students as the result of just a moment or two of visual display cannot be underestimated, particularly when accompanied by student choral reading and effective teacher interpretation. The importance of how a poem "looks" is further demonstrated by showing sequences of poems of different styles, and sequences of the same poem presented as prose poem, in couplets, with varying line breaks, and in other ways meant to highlight the visual effects. I have rediscovered that seventh graders, even in an era of Internet, hypertext, and graphics-enhanced computer pages, are equally fascinated with the technical process of reproducing a book page on a transparency. The students even considered it clever that I placed a poem titled "Bullfrogs" on a green transparency. All of this combines to gather a classroom of vibrant minds momentarily together in time and place. After that, the poem, those minds, and the teacher must do the work. With that last thought in mind, I render the following examples from my 55 minutes with this seventh-grade class.

Class Discussion of "Bullfrogs"

I gave the class a reflective moment to study the poem, observing their rapt attention, listening to them read aloud spontaneously in twos and threes, listening to their comments of "cool," "gross," and "uuuhhhg." Some spoke to others, pointing to different words or lines on the screen. Some were silent, eyes fixed on the screen, lip-reading the words. Some wore puzzled expressions. I did not speak, but observed and listened. All of this lasted 1 or 2 minutes. Then they spoke to me:

One asked, "What is SSSi, SSSiz, whatever?"

"Schlitz," I filled in. "Anyone heard of it?"

"No," the class responded.

"Wanna guess?"

"Something to drink?"

"How do you know that?" I asked.

"Sipping."

I told them outright, "It's a beer. Not much advertised in these parts. What do you know that would fit?"

They speculated possibilities, "Bud Light? Pepsi? Coke?"

"Which?" I teased.

"Bud Light."

"Why?"

"It's a beer. It's on TV. You know, 'I love you man!'"

"What if it didn't have to be a beer?"

"Then Pepsi. No, Coke. I don't know."

"Why not?"

"Well, Pepsi, it sounds better. But Coke, it sounds OK, too, in a way."

We settled on Pepsi because its "p" and "s" sounds fit better with the sounds of "sipping." Few school children in Oklahoma have heard of Schlitz beer, so I use it as a test of reading for meaning. If students ask about it, I assume they are trying to make sense of text. If they do not ask about it, I initiate the questioning. My next move with the class was to go for a substitute word for Schlitz that they knew. Quickly, Bud Light, Pepsi, Coke, and Coors were proposed. We tested each suggestion in the Schlitz slot and it soon became clear to them that the missing alliteration was a problem. The conversation then evolved to how poems make their sounds, to alliteration, to consonance, and to sibilance. We discovered that all three of the choices could work to some degree for different reasons. The class worked in pairs for a moment to address the problem, but we could not think of a brand name that makes sounds that fit as well as Schlitz. Score one for the poet, who wrote in Janeczko's *Poetspeak* (1983), "I don't know if we were actually drinking Schlitz beer, but I like the slurpy, amphibious sound of that word in the first line, along with 'sipping'" (p. 46). Eventually, I shared the poet's comments about writing the poem with the class. Through this problem-solving process, the poem was read aloud many times by individuals discovering the sound patterns in the poem. This group of seventh graders loved to work with sounds. We moved on after approximately 5 minutes, while the interest in the exercise (and the poem) was still high.

I wanted to engage their personal responses while the images were still fresh in their minds. We read the poem again, still without the last line. I asked, "When you are reading the poem, what are you thinking about?" The group exploded. "Frogging. Fishing. Hunting frogs. Messing around at the pond. This TV commercial when these big frogs want beer. When I go shoot frogs with my 22 (gasps of disbelief from the class)." Gradually order was restored and the students told stories of ponds, frogs, fishing, hunting, and eating frog legs, until everyone was well grounded in the potential content of this poem. The class freely offered opinions on the cruelty or pleasures of catching, killing, and delegging frogs and cooking and eating their legs. We proceeded to clarify the most likely literal meanings of the poem and touched lightly on poetics, particularly word choice, the sound and look of poems, line breaks, and nonrhyme, as teachable moments presented themselves, pausing only to help students make images of the more difficult word combinations in the poem, such as "nudging along" and "moss's edge."

I was ready at this point to entice the class to speculate about the title. No one seemed to notice that the title was blocked out. I asked directly, "What would you title this poem?" There were halting answers and unsure answers: "The pond. Creatures from the pond. (R.L. Stine's *Fear Street* series definitely is a part of their personal histories. Some even mentioned him by name in side conversations.) Killing frogs. Bullfrogs." When I revealed the title, "Bullfrogs," there was not much response from the class. Perhaps the title is too plain, too predictable, or not fantastic enough. Interestingly, there was response to the dedication, "- for Ernie, Larry, and Bob." The students asked, "Who are they? Can you do that (dedicate a poem)? They must be the guys hunting frogs." So, the class speculated on the "we" of the second line. "That's why they were drinking beer. They were a bunch of guys out hunting frogs." Now, the class had established a certain wholeness about the poem; we established a speaker and determined who was cutting off the legs.

Hiding the title until the end of the class discussion was an experiment with this age group. I had noticed that not many of their creative writing papers had titles, and it became clear that they needed help with the titling process. I wondered if this level of synthesis was beyond their reach developmentally, whether the level of abstraction was too high, whether they were too concerned about creating intriguing or cute titles, or whether they simply were unpracticed. I thought about possible connections between making titles and deriving titles. Are the mental processes that different? In fact, I have noticed that titles seem to come hard for all age groups, which suggests that this activity requires practice. I concluded that "titling" strategies can be taught, but they would require time.

After the title discussion, I asked the class to read the poem one more time. Then, I read the poem aloud, pausing at the last line, "the moss's edge, looking up at us." I then whisked away the paper blocking the last line, "asking for their legs," and read it with as much dramatic power as I could muster.

Their response was silence. I read the impact in their open eyes. We talked about why the last line grabbed them, why it was separated from the rest of the poem by space, and why it was not even a complete sentence. We discussed how they could break sentences into lines and how they could write that way.

We had read the poem, responded personally, taken it apart as much as the students would bear, then read it aloud again, putting it back together with new meanings. We then talked about the experience of reading the poem.

"Did you like the poem even after discussing it?"

"Yes."

"Is it a good poem?"

"Yes."

"Would you like me to share a few more poems like 'Bullfrogs'? Not to study; just to see them, read them, and hear them?"

"Yes."

So for the next 10 minutes we read poems for the pure enjoyment of it, among others, "The Red Wheelbarrow" and "This Is Just To Say" by William Carlos Williams, and "Jog" by John Ciardi.

To close the class session, I showed a green transparency of a cartoon (Larsen, 1990) depicting three bullfrogs on a stage in appropriate blues band costume playing and singing the "greeeeeeens." Featured in the cartoon is the following "greeeeeeens" lyric:

> My baby's left my lily pad,
> my legs were both deep fried,
> I eat flies all day and when I'm gone
> they'll stick me in formaldehyde...Oh,
> I got the greeeeeeens, I got
> the greens real baaaaaad....

The students laughed, sang the song in small groups, asked about formaldehyde, and asked if they could write poems, stories, and songs. We talked about the reddds, the purrrrples, and all of their favorite colors and the feelings they associate with them. Then we wrote quickly and read aloud as we could, with real voice. I discovered a fair number of the class knew blues music, made the connection, and understood the satire. This was another opportunity to see poetic language, absorb poetics, and internalize through writing the form.

Poetics in Middle School and Secondary Education

So how much poetics should we teach in secondary education, and how do we teach it? Perhaps William Carlos Williams, in his autobiographical piece, *I Wanted to Write a Poem* (1958), provides a clue. He writes that compiling *The Complete Collected Poems of William Carlos Williams 1906–1938* "gave me the whole picture, all I had gone through technically to learn about the making of a poem" (p. 65). He also writes, "My models, Shakespeare, Milton, dated back to a time when men thought in orderly fashion. I felt that modern life had gone beyond that; our poems could not be contained in the strict orderliness of the classics" (p. 65). Williams then discusses *Paterson, Book Two* (1948) as "a milestone for me. One of the most successful things in it is a passage in section three of the poem which brought about—without realizing it at the time writing—my final conception of what my own poetry should be..." (p. 80). It appears that one of the most acclaimed American poets learned his craft over a lifetime of reflection and practice, and believed that writers of the present should not restrict themselves to the poetic forms of times past.

As Williams suggests, understanding and skill in poetics is learned through reading and writing poems over time and through much practice. Certainly, if experienced poets take a lifetime to learn their craft, then we as teachers in our much shorter time with students must learn to be patient in our expectations of student learning of poetics, and of poetry reading and poetry writing. My argument in this chapter is that the most effective place to begin the poetry education of students at middle school and secondary school levels is the "modern life" referred to by Williams, the present. I believe that we should allow students to become comfortable with reading and writing poems close to personal experience and understandable language before they seriously undertake the study and writing of more traditional poetic forms. Blues lyrics, Found Poems, and poems similar to "Bullfrogs" are but three examples of content and form taken from "modern life." Equally important to my argument are teaching approaches that value student experience, personal expression, and learning by doing, and that work from whole to part, that nurture, that minimize the pressure to rote learn poetry facts disconnected from the realities of poetry reading and poetry writing. Early learning of poetics in particular should concentrate on poetic understanding derived from pleasurable poetry reading and poetry writing. This does not mean our expectations should be low, but that they should be realistic.

Understanding and applying poetics involves a complex set of strategies acquired through direct teaching and incidental learning. We should allow for both. At best, our students would leave high school with an appreciation of poetry, with an approach behavior to reading and writing it, and with some grounding in poetics to develop over time.

Author's Note

I gratefully acknowledge the kindness and expertise of Linda Kramer, English teacher at Central Mid-High in Norman, Oklahoma, USA, for allowing me access to her classroom, her time, and, most of all, her students, who demonstrate daily their creative capacities. To them a special acknowledgment for allowing me to use their work: Kathleen Gardenhire, Nick Sanders, Stephanie Hayes, and the most prolific, "Anonymous," whom our exhaustive efforts have yet to identify.

References

Bradbury, R. (1953). *Fahrenheit 451*. New York: Ballantine Books.

Dunning, S., & Stafford, W. (1993). *Getting the knack: 20 poetry writing exercises*. Urbana, IL: National Council of Teachers of English.

Janeczko, P. (1983). *Poetspeak: In their work, about their work*. Scarsdale, NY: Bradbury Press.

Larsen, G. (1990). *The far side*. New York: Farworks.

Preminger, A. (Ed.). (1974). *Princeton encyclopedia of poetry and poetics* (Enlarged edition). Princeton, NJ: Princeton University Press.

Williams, W.C. (1958). *I wanted to write a poem*. Boston, MA: Beacon Press.

Strand Two

Using Writing and Speaking
to Study Language

CHAPTER 4

Language Secrets from a First-Year Teacher in a Rural School

ANTHONY KUNKEL

The principal had warned me that I would be teaching in a very poor community when he hired me. Kids are kids, I thought; deep down they all want to learn. The principal had been hired the previous year to rebuild a high school that currently was rated among the worst in the United Stated. Finding successful, experienced teachers to work in this low paying, rural community in the southeastern United States was a challenge, so he pursued recent graduates who were looking for their first teaching job—new teachers with new ideas. I was hired to teach the new ninth-grade experimental writing classes; the traditional English I had been replaced with Writing I and II.

Assessing the Need to Write

I began the school year with aspirations and expectations not uncommon to most first-year teachers; I was going to make a difference. For the class's first writing assignment I asked the students to write a one-page summary of what they did for their summer vacation—the only requirement (aside from the length) was that they tell a lie. I wanted to see what types of imagination I was working with. The majority of the males wrote stories about fishing trips where they "caught the big one," or about successful hunting adventures that ended with the kill of a 16-point buck. The females, on the other hand, wrote love stories in which they met the perfect man and fell in love. One aspect of the love stories that surprised me was how most of them involved the writer's fighting another girl to be with the man of her dreams. The purpose of the imaginative essay was twofold: First I wanted to see what was relevant in the students' lives, and second, I wanted to assess their competence as writers. I would not have believed the results even if I had been warned. By the end of the first week it became apparent why the principal felt there was a need for a writing program.

Many of the students were spelling the word *t-h-e* by writing *t-h-a*. The common spelling of "think" and "thing" was *t-h-a-n-k* and *t-h-a-n-g*. "There" was spelled *t-h-a-r*. Although I never have been a master speller myself, I was amazed at the inability of these young high school students to spell even the simplest words. It was apparent they were spelling words the way they sounded in their strong southern dialect. The spelling concerned me, but what concerned me more was that most of them never had heard of a comma or period.

After I had read all the students' essays and tried to write positive comments on each, I decided to go to the grammar textbook for an intensive lesson on sentence structure. I thought that if I could get the class to understand how the sentence works, they would be writing like college graduates by the time they finished my class. I could have saved myself a lot of time if I had forgotten I ever found those textbooks.

I had planned the lesson—we would work on the definition of a sentence, then we would work on run-on sentences, then sentence fragments, and by that time the class would be ready to unstring the stringy run-on sentences that could be shortened. After that, we could study subordinating conjunctions and where to place them. I became obsessed with teaching the class about sentences. I gave quizzes that most students failed; I gave homework that none of them did; and I threatened them with tests, which I followed by giving tests. Eighty percent of the class failed these tests.

I decided it was time to call some parents. After all, I thought that is what a good teacher is supposed to do when a student is failing his or her class. When the principal had told me the school was in a very poor community, I had not understood exactly what he meant. I was not prepared for some of the parents I encountered. I did not stop to consider that many of the parents had dropped out of high school, so homework and study skills were not a family priority. After about five disheartening phone calls, I sat and stared at the paper I was holding with the names and phone numbers of the parents. This was not how teaching was supposed to be. I realized at that moment that perhaps I was the one who was not learning anything.

When my first-period class arrived the next day, I told them to put their textbooks away—they would not be needing them for awhile. I told everybody to get out a piece of paper and something to write with. Then, I opened the back door to the classroom, told the students to follow me, and walked out. The classroom exploded in excited talking, desk sliding, and something I had not heard in my class before: laughter. They almost flew out the door; they could not get outside quickly enough. When the entire class was outside, I motioned for them to follow me, and I began walking past several other classes, out to the softball field that was close by.

In the distance I could hear traffic on the highway. I could also hear the physical education class on the football field several hundred yards away. The trees that surrounded the softball field were alive with insect sounds, and it seemed I could hear every one of the excited whispers of my students. I stopped in the middle of center field and faced my class. I looked at their faces one by one, and for the first time in my short career as a teacher, every one of my students was looking at me and paying attention. I pointed to one of the students and said, "Clayton, what do you hear?"

Clayton looked around cautiously, then answered, "What do you mean?"

"I mean, what sounds do you hear right now?" I replied.

He looked around once more, scratched his head, and said, "Well, I reckon I hear cars on the highway."

"Good!" I said so loud that many of the students jumped. "Now write that down and put a period at the end of it."

"Write what down, Mr. K?" Clayton asked.

"Write down, 'I reckon I hear cars on the highway,' period, just the way you said it," I explained.

Some of the students were beginning to look at me suspiciously. I pointed to one of the female class members.

"Amy, what do you hear?" I asked.

"I hear Coach L yelling at someone," she answered.

"Excellent! Write that down and put a period at the end," I instructed.

I pointed to different students, one after another, and asked them what they heard, saw, smelled, and felt. We walked along the perimeter of the fence behind the school, and I instructed them to write down anything they thought no one else would notice. I emphasized that they were to begin each sentence with "I hear" or "I see," and to end the sentence with a period. I did this exercise with all my classes that day and collected their papers at the end of each class. When I read through their papers at the end of the day, I noticed that they all had done the assignment, and that some students had done more than I asked.

The next day I returned the papers to the students and called on different class members to read their work aloud. They were shy at first, but enjoyed reading the sentences they had created in our "outdoor classroom." Some of the more creative students had invented monsters in the trees and some even had used descriptive writing, and when they read their sentences, the other students seemed receptive and amused. I was surprised at the questions and comments the students had for one another. Although the less imaginative students scribbled only a minimal number of words, still they were participating in the readings. After a frustrating beginning to the school year for both my students and me, it had taken only two days to get the students responding, participating, enjoying themselves, and learning.

Implementing a Cooperative Learning Activity

Because my class and I had some momentum, I decided to try a cooperative learning activity. First I put the students into groups of three or four (it is important to note that each group had at least one of the stronger writers of the class placed in it). I then put a prompt on the chalkboard:

It was a dark and stormy night.

As soon as I finished writing the prompt on the board, the class came to life with questions. I instructed each group that they would be writing a short story, one sentence at a time. First, each group was to select one student to begin writing. These students were to copy the prompt from the board and follow it with a sentence of their own. Once they had finished their sentence, they were instructed to pass it to the left.

Next, the people on the left in the groups who were handed the paper were to read what was written and follow it with a sentence of their own. I instructed them that each sentence was to be the next sentence in the group's story, so they could not write about something different, but they were welcome to take the story in any direction they liked.

Lastly, I informed the groups that because they would be reading their stories aloud, it would be necessary for their sentences to flow smoothly. I instructed them that if they found errors in a paper that was passed to them, they should pass it back to the person who wrote it and show them how to make the corrections.

What happened next was nothing short of a miracle. Some students were leaning over their peers' shoulders to watch them write. Others were reading what had been written and started to laugh. Hands began to go up, and I heard comments like, "Is this a fragment?" "Should a comma go here?" and "This just doesn't sound right. What do you think?" As I walked around the classroom to offer assistance, I noted groups in which one student would hand back the paper to another and point at something, or one student would be erasing while another was nodding her head. The whole time stories continued to grow.

With 15 minutes of class left, I told students to pass around the stories one last time. For the last pass, they were to put an ending on their stories. Many of them protested that they were just getting started. I promised the class that we would do a collaborative story again another time, smiling at the idea of promising them more work. After writing the endings, each group selected a reader, and when called, the readers shared their stories with the class. The students turned into eager listeners. When one group would finish, another group could be heard whispering to one another, making comments like "Ours is better." Remarkably, the stories flowed together well, leaving me speechless at the display of imagination and creativity.

I did the same cooperative activity for the next two days, only with different prompts. By the third day, students were writing twice as much. As their stories became better, the competition among groups intensified and I found that, not only were the stories beginning to get entertaining, they also were beginning to be well written.

The success of the cooperative activities in my classroom resulted in the pleasant transformation I had read about in college. My room was becoming a writing community. The students were writing willingly and practically insisting that they be allowed to share their writing. For many of them, everything they wrote was in competition with the other writers in the class. The quieter students would approach me during an assignment, hand me a piece of paper, and look at me expectantly. In many cases the spelling was awful, the sentences were convoluted, and the punctuation was nonexistent. Sometimes, as I looked at the students, I realized that if I criticized their writing in any way, they might stop writing completely. So, when I would look at the paper and read what they actually had written, I would read it as if the spelling and punctuation did not matter. More often than not, I found something worthwhile had been written. I learned to try always to point out something I liked about their writing. With a few kind words, the shy students would almost float back to their desks and sit and stare at their papers as if they were magic. They then would begin writing with complete abandon, their lips moving silently, their heads nodding to the rhythm of their words. I learned never to underestimate the power of positive reinforcement.

New Ideas Do Not Go Unnoticed

It was sometime around the third month of school when the head of the English department called me into her room. It had been brought to her attention that I was not using my textbook, and that I was not teaching grammar or spelling skills. My defense was simple—I told her I was teaching my students to write. She asked me what good their writing was if they could not punctuate appropriately. What she was asking me was something I was worried about myself. I knew that if I stressed grammar they would stop writing, and I was not willing to lose them yet. I told her that I was letting them get their feet wet in writing, building their confidence, and that I had planned to deal with grammar later. Although she expressed support for my ideas, she informed me that I was to confer with the other ninth-grade writing teacher and come up with identical lesson plans and semester and final exams.

I left this meeting feeling like I had been told to conform and sent on my way. I then followed the only logical plan of action I could think of: I stormed into the principal's office and ranted about this injustice. Once the principal had calmed me enough to determine what I was talking about, he set the matter straight. This is when I learned a valuable lesson about living in a small community: Nothing goes unnoticed.

While I had been in my classroom trying to turn my students into budding creative writers, the community had been talking. Because I was new to the area and I still was an outsider, they had not talked to me personally, but instead had talked to the principal, school board members, and other teachers. Overall, what they had been saying was good. Many students were taking their writing home and sharing it with their parents, relatives, and friends. This was good public relations for a school trying to rebuild its reputation. Apparently it was refreshing for members of the community to see students interested in academics.

The principal agreed that the English chair had some valid concerns, but he felt my class was fine the way it was, and he did not share her reservations. He did recommend that I try to share some of my ideas with the other ninth-grade writing teacher. I agreed with him, thanked him, and went straight to the writing teacher's room.

What I found in this teacher was an ally and a friend I had not expected to find. For the first time in my professional teaching career, I found someone with whom to share my enthusiasm and ideas. She was open minded and was receptive to new possibilities for the English curriculum. In addition, because sponsoring the yearbook was taking up all her planning time, my ideas were especially welcome. Sharing my teaching strategies allowed me to feel more a part of the school.

Focusing on the Mechanics

I still needed to address what the English chair had brought up in our meeting. I realized that at some point I did need to deal with the poor spelling and grammar exhibited by my students. Because I had noticed many of the students were beginning to sneak in commas and periods in their writing (where they had not before), I decided to address spelling first.

Activities to Improve Spelling and Vocabulary

During my first year, I had gotten in the habit of writing each day's writing activities on the chalkboard first thing in the morning. I began to intentionally misspell words, because one thing I learned quickly was that students love to see their teachers make mistakes. It did not take long before my spelling mistakes were pointed out to me. When one student would tell me I misspelled a certain word, I would circle it, and emphasize the fact that I was a terrible speller in college.

"But why did you circle it, Mr. K?" my students would ask.

I answered, "Oh that? That's how I got through college. Every time I didn't know how to spell a word, I'd circle it so I could go back and look it up later."

I began by recommending this technique at first, telling the students to be sure to circle the words they were not sure of, then I began to require it. The results were amazing. On major writing projects, short stories, reflective essays, and research writing, I would see rough drafts with countless words circled, crossed out, and rewritten. However, on the final clean copy, very few words would be misspelled. It was becoming second nature for many of my students to circle words as they wrote. As a result, I think that many of them were becoming better spellers. At least they began to think about spelling and lost some inhibitions about identifying potential errors.

Another activity I created to help with spelling was a game called *Vocab War* (see Figure 1). For some time I had been trying to think of a way to replace the traditional vocabulary lessons. As was the case with my textbook unit on sentences, the students simply were not interested in studying vocabulary words. This left me with two options: I could continue assigning vocabulary words and giving them Fs when they would not study them, or I could come up with a new approach to teaching vocabulary. I had learned from my first month in the classroom not to take their poor study habits personally. So instead of settling for a classroom full of Fs, I began thinking of new ways to teach vocabulary.

As Figure 1 indicates, the game requires a rather verbose explanation, but the students catch on quickly. By the third time I played the game in my class, the students wasted no time getting out the dictionaries and organizing themselves. The game did not begin with this many rules and ways to score, but its success forced some changes. What surprised me most about Vocab War was the way my classes began to compete with one another. I now have a permanent score-

FIGURE 1: Vocab War

Objectives
Students will increase vocabulary.

Students will learn cognitive reasoning skills.

Students will become proficient in all uses of the dictionary.

Students will learn to use synonyms and antonyms.

Students will increase spelling and pronunciation skills.

Materials
A dictionary of synonyms and antonyms (found in any bookstore), a chalkboard (an overhead may help), chalk for the students to use, erasers, and a classroom set of dictionaries (the more advanced, the better).

Time Needed
One class period (block or regular).

Procedures
(Note: This lesson was developed to replace a more traditional style of teaching vocabulary, and will increase in efficiency only with regular implementation. Recommended frequency is once weekly or biweekly, depending on your school's class schedule.)

Set Up
One full class period will be needed to set up and explain this lesson. A shortened version of the game should be set up on the chalkboard before class. During the first class on this game the teacher should try to accomplish the following: a summary of the use and definitions of synonyms and antonyms, a lesson on the use of dictionaries (pronunciations of words, how to summarize definitions, different definitions for the same word, and parts of speech), and a walk-through on how to play the game.

(continued)

board in my room that gives each class's average every week. I have turned Fridays into Vocab War day for all of my classes, and several students from different classes stop in between their other classes to get a head start on the five key words.

FIGURE 1: Vocab War (continued)

The Game
Using the largest and most accessible chalkboard in the room, set up the game in the following manner.

pithy	fervor	soluable	inauspicious	junction
buoyant	lethargy	tedious	dispersion	concise
lucky	vapid	division	noxious	apathy
serious	vapory	torpor	sublimated	spirit
haste	alliance	laconic	redundant	cumbrous
discord	malign	gracious	coalition	roseate

Five Key Words									
ZEAL		VOLATILE		UNION		TERSE		SINISTER	
S	A	S	A	S	A	S	A	S	A

Of the five key words in the chart, each will have three synonyms (S) and three antonyms (A)—these are to come from the 30 words listed in the five columns. The idea is simple: each student is responsible to look up and define the five key words. Then the groups should divide the columns and each member begins looking up his or her respective column. Instead of spending time writing down each of these definitions, the students should consult the definitions of the five key words and begin reasoning where each word belongs; this is best done one word at a time. For example, take a look at the first word in the first column of synonyms and antonyms, *pithy*. The dictionary defines this word as "precise and meaningful." Now, with the dictionary in front of you, still on *pithy*, refer to the written definition of the first key word, *zeal* (this is why each member must write the definitions to the five key words). The definition of this word should be something like this: *Enthusiasm, or devotion to a cause.* At this point the students must begin reasoning whether the definition they currently are reading for *pithy* is

(continued)

FIGURE 1: Vocab War (continued)

the same as, or opposite of, the definition they have for *zeal*. If the students cannot match it, they move on to the second key word, *volatile*, and repeat the reasoning and matching process. For *pithy*, the proper match would be a synonym for *terse*, which means *Brief and to the point*. This should be done a word at a time until the students have matched all their words, even if the game has begun. No students should say they are done until their whole group has matched all the words (which rarely happens). At one point the group should begin collaborating to see which words they have matched and which words they still need to find a place for. It is best to give the students about half the class time to look up and match words—remind them not to stop looking up words just because the game has started.

Playing the Game
For a 50-minute class, 5 key words is the perfect number. A very competitive class will usually finish the game with about 5 minutes to spare. For block schedule classes, the number of words may be increased, or the number of synonyms and antonyms may be increased; either way, more time will be needed to look up words and to play. To start the game, select a group to go first and allow them 1 minute to put one word on the board; any word, anywhere they think it should go, but one word only (Each word put up correctly is worth one point. There is no penalty for wrong words; they just do not have any point value). Once the students have put a word under a column and have taken their seats, call the next group. (Do not tell any group if they are right or wrong; only watch as they put their word on the board).

When the next group goes to the board, they may ask to erase a word they think is under the wrong column or is misspelled. In order to do this, they must pronounce the word they wish to erase. If the word they wish to erase is in the right place or if they pronounce it incorrectly, they must take their seat and forfeit their turn—it is best to tell them if they pronounced it incorrectly. If they identify a word and can pronounce it correctly, they are told they may erase it (they may erase only one

(continued)

FIGURE 1: Vocab War (continued)

word a turn). Once they erase a word, they may put any word they like on the board, wherever they like; they do not have to replace the word they erased. If they get to erase a word and then put a word on the board correctly, they get two points instead of one. If they correctly erase a word, but fail to put the word in its proper place (or spell it incorrectly), they receive zero points.

As the Game Progresses
As the game moves forward, students will begin to fill each of the synonym and antonym columns. When a column is complete with the three proper synonyms or antonyms, tell students to circle it (there are no extra points for circling a column; it is only to let them know it is complete). This lets the students know that the words all are correct, or that something is wrong. The more aggressive groups will pounce on an uncircled column with three words, hoping for a two-pointer.

Penalties
The only penalties in the game result either from lack of effort or from not paying attention. If a group at any time passes when it is their turn, a "–1" goes in their grade box (see scoring and grading). Also, if a group puts a word on the board that already is in a circled column, they get a "–1" in their grade box. These negatives come off their score and will affect the class average (if you have classes competing with other classes, they will help motivate their peers).

Scoring and Grading
Scoring is simple. If a group puts a word in the proper column, the group number goes next to that word on the teacher's score sheet. If a group erases a word and puts a word on the board correctly, their number goes next to the word and their number is circled. When the game is over, each group's score is added. Each group number next to a word equals one point and each circled number equals two points. To compensate for classes that play competitive games in which fewer two-pointers are available, each group with a perfect game has its score doubled (this will matter only if you have different periods competing with

(continued)

FIGURE 1: Vocab War (continued)

one another). To keep track of perfect games, a simple "X" can be put in a group's score box when they have a mistake. No group with an "X" in their box can have its score doubled. After all scores have been determined, they are written in the group's score box (any negatives are subtracted at this time), and the winner is announced. Following is an example of the teacher's scoring and grading sheet. This also is the answer and planning sheet that is used to set up the game:

ZEAL   S-fervor, spirit, haste A-lethargy, apathy, torpor.

VOLATILE   S-buoyant, vapory, sublimated A-soluble, serious, cumbrous

UNION   S-junction, coalition, alliance A-dispersion, division, discord

TERSE   S-concise, pithy, laconic A-tedious, vapid, redundant

SINISTER   S-inauspicious, noxious, malign A-lucky, roseate, gracious

	1st period	2nd period	3rd period	4th period	5th period	6th period
group #1						
group #2						
group #3						
group #4						

This enthusiasm is from students who, before taking this class, would not touch a dictionary to save their lives.

Activities to Improve Writing

With the success of the writing activities and the realization that my students were willing to write extensive pieces, I decided to work on writing techniques I thought would help them with their academic papers for other classes. I knew that they had their science projects coming up, so I decided to allow them the opportunity to write them in my class.

We spent a good deal of time in the library, studying where to find research, how to find it, and how to document it. Many students complained because they felt one science class was enough, but in the end most saw the logic of what I was doing and showed a willingness to learn and do the work. The science papers progressed satisfactorily, but a common problem I noticed was that the students did not know how to get from one subject to the next within a paper. They did not know how to use transitions between paragraphs.

I gave this problem some thought and decided to try a cooperative activity with transitions. The results again were almost unbelievable. What is amazing is that getting students to use transitions properly took only half a class period. The activity I developed was called *Rapid Transitions* (see Figure 2).

FIGURE 2: Rapid Transitions

Cooperative learning activity
Groups of three or four are required.

Objective
Students will learn to use (and recognize) transitions for the purpose of connecting sentences and creating unity in their writing.

Approximate time needed
One (50-minute) class period.

Procedures

Step one
The teacher should set up the lesson by writing a variety of transitional words and phrases on either the chalkboard or overhead.

Step two
The teacher should give a brief lecture on transitions, their purpose, and effectiveness.

(continued)

FIGURE 2: Rapid Transitions (continued)

Step three
Instruct all groups that they will need enough paper for each individual, as well as one page for the group. Students will write their names on their individual papers, and write any number between one and seven next to their name; no group may have two of the same number. After their names and numbers are on their papers, groups should be instructed to write their names vertically on their group papers, with their individual numbers beside each name.

Step four
Instruct students that their number will be called and their assignments will be read aloud. As assignments are read, students will write their assignments at the top of their individual paper.

Step five
One student in each group is instructed to begin writing an essay on their assigned topic, only they are told to pass the paper to the left when they have completed two sentences. The person on the left who gets the essay will use one of the example transitions from the chalkboard to bring the essay to their own topic, and then he or she will write one sentence on that topic. Each person may write only two sentences, one a transition, and one about the assigned topic. Based on the number of groups in the class, the passing of the paper should continue until there is only enough time for each group to read aloud their papers. All students should be instructed to work on their own essay while waiting for the group paper to come around—this will also give them ideas so the group paper can move smoothly.

Step six
All groups are instructed to designate a reader to give the group's oral presentation.

Note: If a teacher wishes to grade the assignment, the oral presentations provide an easy way to determine if the transitions are being used appropriately.

(continued)

FIGURE 2: Rapid Transitions (continued)

Rapid Transitions role assignments

1. Your job is to describe the proper way to eat an ice cream cone on a hot day.
2. Your job is to give instructions on the best way to pick up a guy or girl.
3. Your job is to tell what the world will be like in the year 3000.
4. Your job is to convince us that cheerleading should be an Olympic sport.
5. Your job is to tell what you want for Christmas, and why you should get it.
6. Your job is to convince us that this country would have less violence if everybody carried a gun.
7. You just saw a dress in the mall that you must have. Your job is to describe the dress, and tell why you would look good wearing it.

Conclusion

As far as addressing grammar in my classroom, it has turned out to be the least of my problems. Cooperative activities, in which all students are required to write, work well. I spend a great deal of time dividing classes into groups, and I do not hesitate to make changes if I feel a certain group is unproductive. When the group writes, I ask that all group members check the grammar before they turn in an assignment, and I ask that those who make the errors be shown how to fix them. For me, putting students into cooperative groups has been more effective in teaching writing, spelling, and grammar than any textbook could ever be.

Although many of my ninth-grade students are only beginning to write at the ninth-grade level, the distance they traveled over the course of a single year is immeasurable. All of my students have surprised themselves with the quality of their own work at one time or another. The moment they recognize that they have written something worthwhile— something that moves the reader in the way that they intended—they transform from being lazy, oppositional students into willing learners. I have found that most discipline problems disappear when the class is active and engaged. When students are interested, it seems that they cannot learn fast enough. Miraculously, my students now show up before and after school with questions about language and writing. Perhaps the real secret to teaching language and effective writing is letting the students show us how.

CHAPTER 5

Linguistic and Sociolinguistic Requisites for Teaching Language

WALT WOLFRAM

Language arts instruction currently is caught in a dilemma. On the one hand, there is a widespread movement within the profession to eliminate the study of language structure as a topic in its own right. In fact, the National Council of Teachers of English (NCTE) has gone so far as to resolve that "isolated grammar and usage exercises not supported by theory and research is a deterrent to the improvement of students' speaking and writing..." (*Language Arts*, 1986, p. 103). In some circles, grammar study, the tradition most associated with the scrutiny of language structure per se, now is viewed as little more than a set of deductively based, taxonomic classification exercises of questionable educational value (Cleary & Lund, 1993). Instructional focus on the structure of language clearly is in a state of decline.

On the other hand, the increasingly multicultural composition of the language arts classroom exhibits more linguistic diversity than ever before. Students use a wide range of nonmainstream English language structures to reflect their diverse sociolinguistic identities. Traditionally, variant language forms have been viewed simply as imperfect renditions of a more perfect standard and therefore have been seen as targets for eradication in language arts instruction. Over the past several decades, however, sociolinguistic research has indicated that variant language structures are highly systematic in their structure, following linguistic patterning that makes them *linguistically different* rather than *linguistically deficient* forms of English. In a spirit of multicultural inclusion aimed to combat the traditional disregard for socially disfavored dialects of English in the classroom, the College Composition and Communication subdivision of NCTE (1974) set forth a policy statement that "affirm[s] strongly that teachers must have the experiences and training that will enable them to respect diversity and uphold the right of students to their own language" (p. 2).

We thus see, somewhat ironically, that the movement toward eliminating the study of language structure within language arts coincides with a heightened consideration of linguistic diversity in the classroom. Understandably, there is increasing frustration and some confusion within language arts about what instructors and students need to know about language structure and language variation, and why.

In this chapter, I set forth some fundamental linguistic and sociolinguistic requisites for language arts instructors and their students, as well as some practical activities for acquiring this knowledge base. In some respects, the principles offered here are more a matter of perspective than factual knowledge about language, although they involve a foundational knowledge base.

In discussing linguistic and sociolinguistic premises for language study, I take exception to the prevailing notion found in some language arts circles—that the sole reason for studying language structure is to make students more effective speakers and writers. There are scientific, sociohistorical, and humanitarian reasons apart from any utilitarian motivation that justify the examination of language structure. In this respect, language study should be ascribed the same status as other fields of inquiry; it should be committed to a search for fundamental truth about laws of nature and matter. Unfortunately, in the study of language structure and variation, there has been a tolerance of misinformation that is matched in few subject areas. Myths about the structure of language, the basis of language variation, and the socioeducational implications of language variation are rooted deeply in language arts education, and they need to be confronted as honestly as any other unjustified set of beliefs in any other discipline.

This is not to say that understanding the nature of language differences is incompatible with mainstream education goals. In fact, as students learn to pay attention to details of language structure and variation and even learn to manipulate selected patterns from other dialects of English, they will become more equipped to transfer these skills to other language-learning tasks, including the acquisition of a standard variety for mainstream social and educational functions.

Linguistic and Sociolinguistic Premises

Following is a limited set of fundamental premises about language structure that are essential for language arts instruction. Included in each section are sample activities that can be used to guide students in understanding the concepts presented. Most of the proposed activities have been used, with slight adjustments, in teaching a wide range of students—from elementary students as low as fourth grade through graduate students in English who are grappling with fundamental notions of language structure and language variation. Thus, the activities are appropriate for both students and teachers.

An Understanding of Descriptive Grammar Versus Prescriptive Grammar

One of the most fundamental distinctions necessary for language study involves the difference between the *prescriptive* and *descriptive* traditions of grammar study. Prescriptive grammar focuses on the social standards governing how language is supposed to be used. These often are stated in the form of prohibitions such as "do not use *hopefully* as a sentence adverb" (for example, *Hopefully, you'll read this chapter*); "do not use double negatives" (for example, *She don't like nothing I write*); or "do not use double modals" (for example, *You might could read this chapter*). In prescriptive grammar, authorities on language use set the norms, or "rules," for how we should use a mainstream, standard language.

Descriptive grammar, on the other hand, aims to describe the grammatical system of a language as it is used among an actual group of speakers. The emphasis is on what is, not on what should be. Furthermore, the data for this description is ordinary, everyday language. From a descriptive perspective, structures stigmatized by the prescriptivists would be included as long as they were used within the speech community under consideration.

In the case of *hopefully* as a sentence adverb cited earlier, we see a contrast between the informal use of English, even by most speakers whom we would consider "standard," and an older, conservative use of the form that has changed over the years. In the second case of prescriptive prohibition, we find a contrast between a widespread, socially stigmatized multiple negation structure found in a wide range of vernacular English varieties but not in the formal speech of most speakers of English. The descriptive patterning of this vernacular structure is fairly well described by sociolinguists;

the patterns governing negation in vernacular dialects simply are different from those governing negation in standard English. In the third case, there is a contrast between a regional dialect variant—found in a number of southern United States regional dialects—and the typical nonsouthern speaker.

Within prescriptive and descriptive traditions, the notion of "rule of grammar" is quite different. For prescriptive grammar, a rule is defined with respect to social norms, not linguistic composition. For descriptive grammar, a rule is defined in terms of the usage pattern as found for a group of speakers.

The distinction between prescriptive and descriptive grammar is absolutely critical for understanding how language is structured and how language may be examined in a systematic, rigorous way. The distinction also is essential for anyone who confronts linguistic diversity in the classroom. It is difficult to see how instructors genuinely can respect students' language capability and potential if students' language variation is viewed only from a prescriptive viewpoint—a set of rule violations with no intrinsic patterning.

Acknowledging the descriptive perspective on language and language variation provides a basis for respecting language patterning regardless of cultural background or status. This perspective also opens the opportunity to examine language as a unique form of human knowledge. We can uncover the inner knowledge that guides the patterning of all language only if we assume a descriptive perspective. Furthermore, understanding the descriptive perspective also provides a framework for treating the full range of students' language differences in spoken and written language more equitably, certainly a reasonable goal for a multicultural classroom.

The prescriptive-descriptive distinction serves further as a foundation for understanding the essential difference between *linguistic grammaticality* and *social acceptability*. *Grammaticality* is a technical linguistic notion that refers to the fact that languages show systematic, precise linguistic patterning. These patterns, or rules, have their reality in speakers' minds. The key to specific rules is found in the orderly use of items by speakers following their intrinsic cognitive schema. Thus, socially disfavored English sentences, such as *Sometimes my ears be itching* or *The dog kept a-looking for the cat*, follow rigorous linguistic patterning that is every bit as systematic and organized as their standard counterparts.

For example, a speaker of an *a-* prefixing dialect of English will use a construction like *The dog kept a-looking for the cat* but *not* one like **The good a-looking dog barks too much*. (According to linguistic convention, the asterisk (*) before a sentence indicates that the sentence is not linguistically well formed—that is, it violates the rule governing the structural composition of such sentences in the language.) The first sentence attaching an *a-* prefix is linguistically "grammatical" because it fits the governing pattern—*a-* may occur with *-ing* forms when they function as verbs or adverbs. The second sentence is "ungrammatical" because it does not fit the pattern. The *a-* in the second sentence precedes an adjective, which does not fall within the structural restriction for the attachment of *a-* to an *-ing* word.

Similarly, speakers of African American Vernacular English will use *be* in a sentence like *Sometimes my ears be itching* but *not* in a sentence such as **Right now my ears be itching* because the first sentence refers to a habitual activity (an appropriate semantic context for the use of this form), and the second sentence refers to an instantaneous activity (an unsuitable semantic context). The difference between linguistic grammaticality, the foundation for describing the patterning of linguistic structures, and social acceptability, the socially based judgment of standard language, is a fundamental premise of language description.

Instructional Activities

Several types of instructional activities can be used to lead students inductively toward the separation of social judgments and linguistic well-formedness. Following are a few of these activities. The first activity (see Figure 1), involving the attachment of the vernacular prefix *a-* to forms ending in *-ing*, demonstrates the cognitive, intrinsic base of language patterning. The exercise presents forced-choice sentence pairs: students select the appropriate form for *a-* prefix attachment in each sentence pair. The idea behind the task is to demonstrate that students can make systematic judgments about the grammatical contexts for *a-* attachment, judgments that correspond to its patterned usage. The advantage of this exercise is that all students, regardless of dialect background, will give orderly responses that verify the existence of the grammatical patterning (Wolfram, 1982). I have used this exercise successfully with undergraduate and graduate students, with teachers in inservice teacher training workshops, and with elementary school and secondary school students from fourth through twelfth grade. This version of the activity comes from a dialect awareness curriculum developed for eighth-grade students on the Outer Banks of North Carolina, USA (Wolfram, Schilling-Estes, & Hazen, 1996).

The activity in Figure 1 focuses on the rigorous patterning of a nonmainstream language structure, thus demonstrating that linguistic patterning must be separated from social valuation. It is particularly useful because the student does not have to be a native speaker of an *a-* prefixing dialect to make accurate grammaticality judgments.

Other activities may focus more directly on the distinction between linguistic well-formedness and social acceptability. For example, it is logically possible for a sentence to be categorized in the ways listed on page 89.

FIGURE 1: The Use of A- Prefix

In some rural areas of the United States, particularly in Appalachia, some words that end in -ing can take an a-, pronounced as uh, in front of the word. We call this a- prefix because it attaches to the front of the -ing word. The language pattern or rule for this form allows the a- to attach to some -ing words but not to others. We will try to figure out this fairly complicated rule by looking at the kinds of -ing words a- can and cannot attach to. We will do this using our inner feelings about language. These inner feelings, called *intuitions*, tell us where we can and cannot use certain forms. Our job as linguists trying to describe this dialect is to figure out the reason for these inner feelings and to state the exact pattern.

Look at the sentence pairs in List A and decide which sentence in each pair sounds better for attaching the a-. For example, in the first sentence pair, which sentence sounds better: *A-building is hard work* or *He was a-building a house?* For each sentence pair, choose one sentence that sounds better with the a- by placing an "X" in the appropriate blank.

List A: Sentence Pairs for A- Prefixing

1. a. __ *Building* is hard work.
    b. __ She was *building* a house.
2. a. __ He likes *hunting*.
    b. __ He went *hunting*.
3. a. __ The child was *charming* the adults.
    b. __ The child was very *charming*.
4. a. __ He kept *shocking* the students.
    b. __ The store was *shocking*.
5. a. __ They thought *fishing* was easy.
    b. __ They were *fishing* this morning.
6. a. __ The *fishing* is still good here.
    b. __ They go *fishing* less now.

[Answers: 1b, 2b, 3a, 4a, 5b, 6b]

(continued)

FIGURE 1: The Use of A- Prefix (continued)

Examine each of the sentence pairs in terms of the choices for the *a-* prefix and answer the following questions.

- Do you think there is some pattern that guided your choice of an answer? You can tell if there is a definite pattern by checking with other people who did the same exercise on their own.

- Do you think that the pattern might be related to parts of speech? To answer this, see if there are any parts of speech where you cannot use the *a-* prefix. Look at *-ing* forms that are used as *verbs* and compare those with *-ing* forms that operate as nouns or adjectives. For example, look at the use of *charming* as a verb and adjective in sentence 3.

- Write a rule for *a-* prefixing that explains the pattern found in List A.

The first step in figuring out the pattern for *a-* prefix is related to the part of speech of the *-ing* word. Now let us look at another difference related to prepositions such as *through*, *from*, and *by*. Based on the sentence pairs in List B, say whether or not the *a-* form can be used after prepositions (specifically, those mentioned above). Use the same technique you used for List A. Select the sentence from each sentence pair, and tell which sounds better with the *a-* by placing an "X" in the appropriate blank.

List B: A Further Detail for A- Patterning

1. a. __ They make money by *building* houses.

    b. __ They make money *building* houses

2. a. __ People can't make enough money *fishing*.

    b. __ People can't make enough money from *fishing*.

3. a. __ People destroy the beauty of the mountains through *littering*.

    b. __ People destroy the beauty of the mountains *littering*.

[Answers: 1b, 2a, 3b]   *(continued)*

FIGURE 1: The Use of A- Prefix (continued)

• State the pattern for *a-* prefixing that explains its relation to prepositions such as *from*, *by*, and *through*.

We now have another detail for figuring out the pattern for *a-* prefix use related to prepositions, but there still is another part to the pattern for *a-* prefix use to consider. This time, however, the pattern is related to pronunciation. For the following *-ing* words, try to figure out why the pronunciation makes one sentence sound better than the other. To help you figure out the pronunciation trait that is critical for this pattern, the stressed or accented syllable of each word is marked with the symbol ´. Place an "X" in the blank beside the sentence in each pair that sounds better.

List C: Figuring Out a Pronunciation Pattern for A- Prefix

1. a.__ She was *discóvering* a trail.
    b.__ She was *fóllowing* a trail.
2. a.__ She was *repéating* the chant.
    b.__ She was *hóllering* the chant.
3. a.__ They were *fíguring* the change.
    b.__ They were *forgétting* the change.
4. a.__ The baby was *recognízing* the mother.
    b.__ The baby was *wrécking* everything.
5. a.__ They were *décorating* the room.
    b.__ They were *demánding* more time off.

[Answers:1b, 2b, 3a, 4b, 5a]

Can the *a-* prefix be used when the first syllable of the *-ing* verb is accented? Can it be used when it is not accented? State this pattern.

Now, say exactly how the pattern for attaching the *a-* prefix works, including the three different details from your examination of the examples in Lists A, B, and C, in the space below.

(continued)

FIGURE 1: The Use of A- Prefix (continued)

In List D, show which sentences may attach an *a-* prefix by using your understanding of the *a-* prefix rule and explaining why the *-ing* form may or may not take the *a-* prefix. Write Y(es) if the *a-* prefix can attach to the sentence and N(o) if it cannot in the space provided. Below the sentence, give the reason why the *a-* can or cannot attach to the *-ing* word. **List D: Applying the A- Prefix Rule**

1. ___ She kept *handing* me more work.
2. ___ The team was *remémbering* the game.
3. ___ The team won by *playing* great defense.
4. ___ The team was *playing* real hard.
5. ___ The coach was *charming*.

[Answers: 1. yes, 2. no, 3. no, 4. yes, 5. no]

Sentences can be

- *linguistically grammatical and socially acceptable* in terms of standard language norms (for example, *I'm going to like this class*);

- *linguistically grammatical and socially unacceptable* (for example, *I ain't going to like this here class*);

- *linguistically ungrammatical and socially acceptable* (for example, **My father didn't like me and I didn't even like me*); and

- *linguistically ungrammatical and socially unacceptable* (for example, **The a-charming person likes this class*).

The exercise given in an abbreviated version in Figure 2 works through these notions. This exercise is appropriate for upper-level secondary students and for teachers.

The point of such activities is quite straightforward—to discern operationally the separation of the descriptive study

FIGURE 2: Linguistic Grammaticality and Social Acceptability: Sorting Out the Difference

The notions of linguistic grammaticality and social acceptability may combine in different ways to account for judgments about sentences. For example, there are four logical combinations of social acceptability and grammaticality judgments, as follows:

1. grammatical, socially acceptable
   e.g., *I'm going to like this class.*
2. grammatical, socially unacceptable
   e.g., *I ain't gonna like this here class.*
3. ungrammatical, socially acceptable
   e.g., *My father didn't like me, my mother didn't like me, and I didn't even like me.* (Note: This is ungrammatical because the same referent within a clause should receive a reflexive pronoun, as in *I didn't like myself*, rather than an objective pronoun, as in *I didn't like me.*)
4. ungrammatical, socially unacceptable
   e.g., *The a-charming person likes this class.*

Judge the following sentences in terms of acceptability and grammaticality. Are there any logical combinations that appear to be somewhat questionable? Why? What does this exercise teach you about the popular use of the term "grammatical" as it compares with its technical use by linguists?

1. The instructor handed out the exercise.
2. The instructor handed out it.
3. This exercise is a-relaxing, ain't it?
4. The students kept a-doing the exercise.
5. She always be doing her homework, don't she?
6. She be doing her homework right now, be she?
7. She comes to school by a-taking a bus.

[Answers: (SA = Socially Acceptable; SU = socially unacceptable; G = linguistically grammatical; U = linguistically ungrammatical) 1. SA/G, 2. SA/U, 3. SU/U, 4. SU/G, 5. SU/G, 6. SU/U, 7. SU/U]

of language from social judgments about language derived from the prescriptive tradition of evaluation. Other activities might focus directly on traditional differences between prescriptive rules and descriptive rules, such as the difference between the prescriptive edict about the sentence adverb *hopefully* and its actual use by the vast majority of English speakers.

An Understanding of the Linguistic Integrity of All Language Varieties

An authentic respect for the linguistic integrity of language variation should go hand-in-hand with an understanding of the prescriptive-descriptive distinction discussed earlier. Unfortunately, there is no language arts tradition for examining variation as a part of the study of language. In its place is a tradition for targeting such variation for eradication. Occasionally, discussions of literary caricatures of dialect speakers may arise, but these typically do not include the examination of linguistic patterning. The discussion of language variation as a topic of inquiry remains neglected in the classroom despite the fact that social dialectology over the past several decades has challenged the basic linguistic and sociolinguistic tenets underlying the current treatment of dialects in the education curriculum.

The most effective way to develop an appreciation for the intricacies of language variation involves working through some actual linguistic patterns governing socially disfavored forms. Such an awareness affects not only the perspective of language arts instructors, but also how students feel about other students and themselves. Students who speak socially favored varieties may view their dialectally different peers as linguistically deficient. Worse yet, speakers of socially disfavored varieties may come to accept this viewpoint about their own language. Students, as well as teachers, need to understand that a dialect difference is not an inherent linguistic or cognitive deficit.

Several activities can be used to underscore the intrinsic patterning of all varieties of language. One activity I have used involves the use of "habitual *be*" in African American Vernacular English introduced earlier. As noted previously, "habitual *be*" is used to refer to an activity that recurs intermittently over time, as in *Sometimes my ears be itching*, but is not typically used with instantaneous activities or permanent activities, as in *My ears be itching right now* or *She be my mother*. However, in the case of *be*, unlike the *a*- prefixing construction presented earlier, I have found that only authentic speakers of this vernacular variety intuitively make the correct grammaticality judgments (Wolfram, 1982). That is, speakers of African American Vernacular English will systematically choose the correct use of *be* in a forced-choice sentence selection task, but speakers of other varieties of English, including standard English, will make random selections when given a grammaticality choice between sentences such as *My ears usually be itching* and *My ears be itching right now*.

The dichotomy between native and nonnative dialect speaker intuitions with respect to grammaticality judgments about *be* can be used to show that we cannot assume that the intuitions from our dialect background necessarily apply to other dialects. At the same time, it reinforces our understanding of the intricate, intrinsic basis of patterning. In the activity presented in Figure 3, we anticipate that nonnative speakers of African American Vernacular English will make random choices with respect to the grammaticality of habitual *be* forms in forced-choice sentence pairs, and that this response pattern will differ from speakers who regularly use these forms in a systematic way.

The exercise has been used in various pedagogical venues, ranging from inservice teacher workshops to classrooms of fourth-grade students in large urban areas and in

FIGURE 3: *Be* in African American English

Consider a form found in a dialect that is sometimes used by African American speakers. The form *be* is used where other dialects use *am*, *is*, or *are*, but in this case, *be* has a special meaning. People who use this dialect can tell where it may be used and where it may not. In the sentence pairs below, choose one of the sentences in each pair where *be* seems to fit better. If you are not sure of the answer, simply make the best possible guess. Place an "X" next to the sentence you think is more appropriate for the use of *be*.

1. a.___ They usually *be* tired when they come home.
    b.___ They *be* tired right now.
2. a.___ When we play basketball, she *be* on my team.
    b.___ The girl on the court *be* my sister.
3. a.___ James *be* coming to school right now.
    b.___ James always *be* coming to school.
4. a.___ Wanda usually don't *be* in school.
    b.___ Wanda don't *be* in school today.
5. a.___ My ankle *be* broken from the fall.
    b.___ My ankles *be* itching.

Summarize the results for the class, noting how many students selected each sentence pair. Now consider the responses given by a group of students who regularly use this form as a part of their dialect. The responses given here come from a group of African American students in Baltimore, Maryland, USA. Notice the systematic responses. What rule might explain the patterning of the responses?

1. 32   a. *They usually be tired when they come home.*
    3   b. They be tired right now.
2. 31   a. *When we play basketball, she be on my team.*
    4   b. The girl in the picture be my sister.
3. 4   a. James be coming to school right now.
    31   b. *James always be coming to school.* (continued)

FIGURE 3: *Be* in African American English (continued)

4.	24	a. *Wanda be going to school every day.*
	11	b. Wanda be in school today.
5.	3	a. My ankle be broken from the fall.
	32	b. *Sometimes my ankles be itching.*

As you can see, the students in Baltimore show a clear preference for the use of *be*. Notice how it is used with adverbs like *always* and *usually*, but not with adverbs like *right now* and *today*. This choice of adverb is because *be* typically is used to indicate a regularly occurring activity. Now apply your rule to the following exercises. In the sentences below, write Y in the space provided if the sentence correctly follows the *be* pattern and N if it does not. If your rule is correct, you should have no problem identifying appropriate usage.

1. ___ The students always *be* talking in class.
2. ___ The students don't *be* talking right now.
3. ___ Sometimes, the teacher *be* early for class.
4. ___ At the moment, the teacher *be* in the lounge.
5. ___ Linguists always *be* asking silly questions about language.

[Answers: 1. yes, 2. no, 3. yes, 4. no, 5. yes]

isolated rural areas. It demonstrates inductively how all varieties of languages must be respected for their intrinsic patterning. It demonstrates further that we cannot simply assume cross-dialectal language intuitions. And once again, it reinforces the need to separate the systematic patterning of language from judgments of social acceptability. As presented here, the activity is adapted from the dialect awareness materials my colleagues and I developed for eighth-grade students on the Outer Banks in North Carolina, USA (Wolfram, Shilling-Estes, & Hazen, 1996). For this student population, which is exclusively Anglo American, the presentation assumes that students will not have native-speaker intuitions about the use of habitual *be*.

Similar activities can be undertaken for pronunciation patterning to show how dialect variation is subject to systematic patterning. Figure 4 is an activity focused on the southern U.S. pronunciation pattern in which words like *pin* and *pen* are pronounced identically. In presenting this activity to students, I usually rely on a tape recording of a native speaker of a southern U.S. dialect who produces these words appropriately for this dialect.

It is virtually impossible for teachers and students to engage in language patterning activities without developing an appreciation for the intricacy and exactness of the linguistic patterning in all varieties of English. More importantly, those who engage in these activities realize operationally that grammatical complexity does not respect social position.

The rigorous, systematic study of language differences also exposes students to the investigation of language patterning as a kind of scientific inquiry. In its present form, the study of language in schools has been reduced to laborious, taxonomic exercises such as parts of speech identification, sentence parsing, and other comparable metalinguistic exercises of questionable value. Few students understand this type of inquiry as scientific in the sense that hypotheses are formed based on a particular type of language data and then are confirmed or rejected using a specialized argumentation structure. In the exercises presented in Figures 1 through 4, students hypothesize about certain forms of language and then check them on the basis of actual usage patterns. This process is a type of scientific inquiry into language that generally is untapped in students' present instruction about language. It also involves a higher order thinking skill that is becoming a central goal of current education.

FIGURE 4: Southern U.S. Vowel Pronunciation

In some southern U.S. dialects of English, words like *pin* and *pen* are pronounced the same, and usually, both words are pronounced as *pin*. This pattern of pronunciation also is found in other words. List A has words where the *i* and *e* are pronounced the same in southern U.S. dialects. Listen to the tape of a southern speaker pronouncing the words in List A.

List A: *I* and *E* Pronounced the Same
1. *tin* and *ten*
2. *kin* and *ken*
3. *windy* and *Wendy*
4. *sinned* and *send*

Although *i* and *e* in List A are pronounced the same, other words exist in southern U.S. dialects where *i* and *e* are pronounced differently. List B has word pairs in which the vowels are pronounced differently. Listen to the tape of a southern speaker pronouncing the words in List B.

List B: I and E Pronounced Differently
1. *lit* and *let*
2. *pick* and *peck*
3. *pig* and *peg*
4. *litter* and *letter*

Compare List A and List B and try to determine the rule behind the southern U.S. pronunciation of *i* and *e*. In doing this, look at the sounds that follow the vowels.

• What sound is found after the vowel in all of the examples given in List A?

• Is the same sound found in List B? In the space below, write a rule that explains the pattern of pronunciation of Southern *i* and *e*.

(continued)

FIGURE 4: Southern U.S. Vowel Pronunciation (continued)

Now, see if your rule works by applying it to the words in List C. In the space provided beside each pair of words, write S if the vowels are pronounced the same and D if the vowels are pronounced differently. After you are done, you will hear a southern speaker pronounce the words in List C to check your answers.

LIST C: Same or Different?

____ 1.   *bit* and *bet*

____ 2.   *pit* and *pet*

____ 3.   *bin* and *Ben*

____ 4.   *Nick* and *neck*

____ 5.   *din* and *den*

[Answers: 1. D, 2. D, 3. S, 4. D, 5. S]

Did your rule apply successfully to List C? If not, try to rewrite it so that it does apply.

An Understanding of Different Levels of Organization Within Language

Language is organized simultaneously on several different levels. Traditionally, these include phonology, grammar, and semantics. *Phonology* is concerned with the ways in which sounds are organized, including contrastive sound segments and the patterning of sound combinations in sequences. The example earlier of the *pen-pin* merger before nasal sounds such as *n*, *m*, and *ng* is an example of organization on the phonological level. *Grammar* includes *morphology*, the ways in which the smallest meaning-carrying units of language, *morphemes*, are built into words; and *syntax*, the ways in which words are organized into larger units such as phrases and sentences. (The activity involving the *a-* prefix involves a grammatical pattern.) *Semantics* is concerned with meaning, including the lexicon of a language and the ways in which systematic relationships of meaning are organized within a language. A related area, sometimes considered a level apart from semantics, is *pragmatics*, which is concerned with how the forms of language are used to carry out the particular communicative functions of language in its social setting. In pragmatics, the important issues concern what to say, to whom, when, and where. This component of language is particularly important in developing a more critical understanding of language discourse because a speaker's intentions, or reasons for communicating, are the central focus of inquiry. Inferences and relations between literal and nonliteral meaning typically are treated as a part of pragmatics.

An understanding of the simultaneous organization of language on these various levels is essential for those who examine language structure. It also is important in understanding the ways in which language can vary, and how this variation may be interpreted. Many different types of activities can be offered to engage students in recognizing these levels of language organization. Activities presented earlier in the chapter demonstrate phonological and grammatical patterning; I now will present activities related to lexical variation and pragmatics. The activity presented in Figure 5 focuses on lexical variation in the island of Ocracoke that is quite localized for the Outer Banks of North Carolina. It is offered as a prototype for student involvement in gathering local and regional lexical items rather than an activity to be adopted as given in a different educational setting. Similar exercises have been developed in different regional settings (Wolfram et al., 1996; Wolfram & Creech, 1996). Furthermore, students can take an active role in constructing local adaptations of this exercise. From such an activity, students should become aware of the culturally specific, relative nature of lexical inventories. The activity is adapted from an eighth-grade

FIGURE 5: Vocabulary in Ocracoke

There are several vocabulary differences that can be described for Ocracoke, and each of the uses has a unique history. Some uses can be traced back in the English language over a thousand years, and some go back just a few years. For example, words like *token* (in *token of death*), *mommuck*, and *quamish* were used centuries ago in ways similar to how they are used in Ocracoke today. Other terms such as *dingbatter*, *scud*, and *up the beach* are relatively recent uses. We can trace certain vocabulary forms confidently, but we can make only educated guesses about the origins of other words. For example, a unique Ocracoke use of the phrase *call the mail over* may be traced to the custom of distributing mail by calling aloud the names of those who received letters at the dock when the mail boat arrived. We are not exactly sure how *meehonkey* came into use, but we guess that it had something to do with the attempt to imitate the call of a goose.

Of course, most of the dialect words found in Ocracoke are found in other dialects as well, but a few are found only in Ocracoke. And the use of vocabulary in Ocracoke differs according to the user's age and background. Following is a sample of some of the dialect words that have been collected. As you examine these words, think of the following questions:

Which of these words do you use?

Which of these words do you know? If you don't know the word, who do you think would?

Do you think people from other areas use these words? Where do you think they might use the words?

A Sample of Some Dialect Vocabulary in Ocracoke

Following are a few examples that have been described as a part of the Ocracoke dialect. Use these examples in order to do the exercise that follows.

buck n.   A friend, usually a male friend. *He's a real buck.*

(continued)

FIGURE 5: Vocabulary in Ocracoke (continued)

call the mail over v. ph.	Distribute the mail. Originally comes from the custom of distributing mail by calling aloud the names of those who received letters at the dock when the mail boat arrived. Now used for more general reference to the distribution of mail in the boxes at the post office. *Is the mail called over yet?*
catawampus adj. Also *cattywampus*	In a diagonal position; crooked, not square. *The box was sitting there catawampus.*
dingbatter n.	A nonnative of Ocracoke or the Outer Banks. Sometimes used somewhat negatively to refer to someone who is ignorant of island life. *The dingbatter kept getting his fishing line tangled with mine.*
guano, also *goana, goanner* n.	Fertilizer, often from fowl such as chickens or coastal birds. By extension, it can refer to any type of fertilizer, including commercial fertilizer. Comes from the Spanish term *guano* (from Peru) where it was used to refer to dung from coastal birds. *Did Owen put lots of goanner on his garden?*
miserable 'n the wind adj.	Agitated; feeling very uneasy or unsettled. Very bad. A shortened version of the phrase *miserabler than the wind. Rudy is miserable 'n the wind when he's on his week off from the ferry; The day was miserable 'n the wind.*
mommick Also *mammock, mommuck* v.	To harass or bother. In Shakespeare's day, this term had a slightly different meaning: to break, cut, or tear into fragments or shreds. The sentence, *Young'uns, haint I been mommucked this day?* is a classic island phrase that focuses on some traditionally recognized dialect traits, including the verb *mommuck*.

(continued)

FIGURE 5: Vocabulary in Ocracoke (continued)

slick cam adj.   A very calm water, typically used with refer-
Also   ence to the Pamlico Sound. *It was a slick cam*
slick calm adj.   *out there today.*

An Exercise with Ocracoke Dialect Vocabulary

Following are some words that are part of the Ocracoke dialect vocabulary. For each of the words, do the following:

- Figure out what the word means, if you do not already know. You can usually do this by asking some different island residents of different ages about the words.

- Use the word in a sentence and try to figure out what part of speech it is.

- Identify the type of people who know the word and who use it; Is it used by older people, younger people, by nonislanders?

- Which of the words do you think are used *only* in Ocracoke or in the Outer Banks? Write your answers here.

goodsome

meehonkey

Russian rat

scud

token of death

Ocracoke Dialect Vocabulary Game:
How to Tell an O'Cocker from a Dingbatter

Fill in the blanks in the following sentences, choosing your answer from the list provided. You only have five minutes to complete the worksheet, and you *may not* look at the lexicon or share answers. At the end of five minutes, swap your book with a neighbor to check each other's work. For each correct answer, you will receive 1 point, and for each question missed, you will receive no points. Good luck.

(continued)

FIGURE 5: Vocabulary in Ocracoke (continued)

Word List: across the beach, buck, call the mail over, dingbatter, doast, goaty, goodsome, meehonkey, miserable 'n the wind, mommuck, O'cocker, quamish, Russian rat, say a word, scud, smidget, slick cam, to, up the beach, young 'uns

1. They went _____ to Hatteras to do some shopping.
2. That _____ is from New Jersey.
3. That place sure was smelling _____.
4. Elizabeth is _____ the restaurant right now.
5. I put a _____ of salt on my apple.
6. We took a _____ around the island in the car.
7. They are always together because he is his _____.
8. Back in the old days they used to call hide and seek _____.
9. The ocean was so rough today I felt _____ in the boat.
10. Last night she came down with a _____.
11. I saw a big _____ in the road.
12. That meal last night was _____.
13. When Rex and James Barrie get together they sure can _____.
14. You cannot be an _____ unless you were born on the island.
15. The sea was real rough today; I felt _____ out there.
16. When they _____ I hope I get my letter.
17. She used to _____ him when he was a child.
18. There was no wind at all today and it was a _____ out there on the sound.
19. There was a big, dead shark that they found _____.
20. _____ do not act like they used to back then.

(continued)

FIGURE 5: Vocabulary in Ocracoke (continued)

Put a 1 by all the correct answers and an "X" by all the incorrect answers. Add the correct answers and place the total in the blank. Hand back the workbook to its owner.

number of correct answers _____

Check your number of correct answers against the continuum below.

Place an "X" where you would fall on this continuum.

O'cocker 20 ——— 15 ——— 10 ——— 5 ——— Dingbatter

[Answers: 1. up the beach, 2. dingbatter, 3. goaty, 4. to, 5. smidget, 6. scud, 7. buck, 8. meehonkey, 9. miserable 'n the wind, 10. doast, 11. Russian rat, 12. goodsome, 13. say a word, 14. O'cocker, 15. quamish, 16. call the mail over, 17. mommuck, 18. slick cam, 19. across the beach, 20. Young 'uns]

student workbook on dialect and language variation (Wolfram, et al., 1996).

Other types of activities might focus directly on sorting levels of language organization or on the relation between sentence formation and communicative function. Following are samples of each type of activity. The activity in Figure 6 on page 104, from Wolfram et al. (1996), is geared for upper-elementary levels; the activity in Figure 7 on page 105 is appropriate for upper-level secondary students, where students are more involved in examining literal and nonliteral uses of language.

FIGURE 6: What Kind of Difference Is It?

In the following sentences, decide whether the difference between each pair is at the pronunciation, vocabulary, or grammar level. Place a *P* for pronunciation, a *V* for vocabulary, or a *G* for grammar level difference in the blank provided beside each pair.

1. That *feller* sure was tall.
   That *fellow* sure was tall.

2. She needed a *rubberband*.
   She needed a *gumband*.

3. They usually *be doing* their homework.
   They usually *do* their homework.

4. I *weren't* there yesterday.
   I *wasn't* there yesterday.

5. She drank a *milkshake*.
   She drank a *cabinet*.

6. I asked him *if he was going over the beach*.
   I asked him *is he going to the beach?*

7. The *skeeters* are bad in August.
   The *mosquitoes* are bad in August

8. They didn't do *nothing* yesterday.
   They didn't do *anything* yesterday.

9. They used to *call* the mail on the boat.
   They used to *announce* the mail on the boat.

10. They went *hunting and fishing*.
    They went *a-hunting and a-fishing*.

[Answers: 1. P, 2. V, 3. G, 4. G, 5. V, 6. G, 7. V or P, 8. G, 9. V, 10. G]

FIGURE 7: How to Carry Out a Speech Act

Consider the following sentences that may be used to accomplish the same social action. What is the speaker trying to accomplish? Notice the types of sentences that are used, such as declaratives, imperatives, and questions. What does this exercise show about the uses of these sentence types? Are some types of sentences considered more polite than others? Rank the sentences in order of politeness.

> Pass me the butter!
>
> Can you pass me the butter?
>
> I would like you to pass the butter.
>
> You need to pass the butter.
>
> Would you mind passing the butter?
>
> Are you using the butter?
>
> These potatoes could use some butter.

Consider the possible ways you could get someone to open a window. Include both direct and indirect ways of doing this. What types of sentences can you use to accomplish the same directive? What kinds of structures seem to be more polite than others? Why would a speaker use a different sentence form to accomplish the same social action?

Language Change Is Natural and Inevitable

It is essential to understand the dynamic nature of language. Language change is inevitable, ongoing, and natural. In fact, the only static, stable language is a dead one. Language change can be complex and appear haphazard, but it ultimately is orderly and systematic.

An understanding of the processes of change that the English language has undergone should inform instructors and students on several levels. First, it should provide a basis for understanding the orderly cognitive and behavioral processes that bring about change. For example, through the process of analogy, languages tend to change irregular, minority patterns into regular, dominant ones: "regularization" is a normal and natural change that takes place within language. When students from vernacular backgrounds regularize the past tense of irregular verbs, such as *knowed* for *knew* and *growed* for *grew*, they simply are following a time-honored and natural tradition of leveling irregular forms—the same processes that gave us the regular, now-standard forms of *worked* (once *wrought*) and *help* (once *holp*). Many of the regular verbs we accept as a part of present-day standard English once were irregular forms. Thus, current progress simply follows the principles that have guided language change in the past.

Second, an understanding of the dynamic nature of language change should foster an appreciation for the flexible nature of language. Language is not set permanently, and language change may affect all levels of language in significant ways. In English, for example, we have drastically changed grammatical paradigms, altered significantly the sequencing of words in phrases and sentences, lost sounds, acquired sounds, and radically changed the inventory of lexical items. All these changes are part of a continuously developing language; no language state is structurally superior, just different. An appreciation for how radically the English language has changed over time should at least promote more tolerance for the small types of changes it currently is undergoing.

Finally, an understanding of language change should broaden our views on language standards. Our inclination is to think of language standards as firm and consistent, but history belies this interpretation. For example, during the Middle English period associated with authors such as Chaucer, double negatives, the scourge of many present-day English instructors, were quite acceptable; in fact, this structural pattern was the only way to form certain negative constructions. The social stigmatization of double negatives in sentences

FIGURE 8: The Changing English Language

English has changed dramatically over the centuries. In fact, if we go back far enough, we can barely recognize the language as English. Compare the versions of English at various stages in its history, as found in the first verse of the Lord's Prayer.

Old English (about 950 A.D.)
Fader urer ∂u bist in heofnas, sie gehalgad noma din

Middle English (about 1350 A.D.)
Oure fadir ρat art in heuenes, halwid be ρi name

Early Modern English (about 1550 A.D.)
O oure father which arte in heven, hallowed be thy name

Modern English (about 1985 A.D.)
Our father, who is in heaven, may your name be sacred
        or
Our father, who art in heaven, hallowed be your name

1. Try pronouncing the different versions of English. In the older versions (Old English and Middle English), "silent letters" do not exist, so you will need to pronounce *all* the letters. The symbol ∂ is pronounced something like the *th* of *this*, and the ρ is pronounced like the *th* of *think*.

2. Try to identify some of the older versions of modern words. For example, trace the words that became the current words *father*, *heaven*, *name*, *is*, and *our*. What modern English word, other than *sacred*, did *hallow* become?

3. What does this comparison tell you about the way the English language has changed over the centuries?

such as *She didn't do nothing* is a relatively late sociolinguistic development in the history of English. Furthermore, change in the social status of language items may proceed quite rapidly. Thus, the now-stereotypical New York City *r*-less pronunciation in words like *New Yo'k* (New York) or *fou'* (four) actually was a prestigious pronunciation prior to World War I; its decline in social status has taken place in the latter half of the 20th century. Similar stories can be told for a number of linguistic features that now fill our hallowed inventories of socially stigmatized structures. Certainly, the lessons of language history should teach us that language is much more flexible than our attitudes about it.

The simple comparative activity in Figure 8 on the previous page shows how language can change dramatically over the centuries. By examining a familiar passage, in this case the Lord's Prayer, we can see how language can change radically on every level—in its sounds, its words, and the orderly arrangement of words within sentences.

Conclusion

On one level, the set of sociolinguistic and linguistic principles set forth in this chapter may seem basic, limited, and transparent; however, operationalizing these premises within the language arts curriculum often is another matter. These premises often conflict with traditional ideologies and practices related to language arts education, so that implementing these principles in the language arts classroom sometimes can be quite involved and fraught with controversy. Linguistic equity in the language arts classroom does not come easily. Unfortunately, misinformation about language and language variation is not simply innocent folklore. Substantive socioeducational inequities continue to be perpetuated when these premises are ignored in the classroom. These inequities concern the assessment and categorization of students' language skills and language potential. Furthermore, these premises underlie how instructors feel about students and how students feel about other students and themselves. Therefore, nothing can be more critical to language arts instruction than foundational truths about language and language differences.

References

Cleary, L., & Lund, N. (1993). Debunking some myths about traditional grammar. In L.M. Cleary & M.D. Linn (Eds.), *Linguistics for teachers* (pp. 483–489). New York: McGraw Hill.

College Composition and Communication Committee on Language Statement. (1974). Students' rights to their own language. *College Composition & Communication, 25.* Champaign-Urbana, IL: National Council of Teachers of English.

NCTE to you: Issues, news, and announcements. (1986) *Language Arts, 63,* 103.

Wolfram, W. (1982). Language knowledge and other dialects. *American Speech, 57,* 3–17.

Wolfram, W., & Creech, K. (1996). *Dialects and island speech.* Eighth grade curriculum developed for the Harkers Island School, Harkers Island, NC. Raleigh, NC: North Carolina Language and Life Project.

Wolfram, W., Detwyler, J., & Adger, C. (1992). *All about dialects* (Instructor's manual). Washington, DC: Center for Applied Linguistics.

Wolfram, W., Schilling-Estes, N., & Hazen, K. (1996). *Dialects and the Ocracoke brogue.* Eighth grade curriculum developed for the Ocracoke School, Ocracoke, NC. Raleigh, NC: North Carolina Language and Life Project.

Strand Three

Language Use in Different Academic Settings

CHAPTER 6

The Languages of Words and Numbers

MICAH DIAL AND LAWRENCE BAINES

Although the mere mention of mathematics is enough to strike terror in the hearts of many language teachers, it is a fact that mathematics is a language. Dictionary definitions (Random House, 1992) indicate the connection between the two subjects:

> Mathematics—the systematic treatment of magnitude, relationships between figures and forms, and relations between quantities expressed symbolically.

> Language—any set or system of formalized symbols, signs, sounds, or gestures used or conceived as a means of communicating.

Mathematics, like English or music, is an order of knowledge and a form of communication. All three forms contain symbols and syntax that represent concepts and convey meanings. This chapter reviews previous studies regarding the connection between learning language and learning mathematics, discusses this connection using examples from our work, and offers a few suggestions on how language teachers can enhance the learning of both language and mathematics.

The Connection Between Learning Language and Learning Mathematics

Evidence exists that supports the connection between learning language and learning mathematics. For example, it has been shown that the greater a student's ability to read and write, the greater his or her comprehension of mathematics is likely to be (Maida, 1995). In the classroom, however, the connection between language and mathematics often goes unrecognized. In fact, the two subjects often are presented as opposing systems.

Vocabulary is an important element in learning mathematics, and language teachers often rely on mathematics teachers and textbooks to teach words and concepts such as addition, subtraction, sum, equals, volume, and degrees (Monroe, 1995; Stauffer, 1966). Math teachers at the secondary level often must teach the vocabulary of basic arithmetic because many teachers at the elementary level do not teach proper vocabulary (Capps & Pickreign, 1993; May, 1995; Parker, 1995; Tracy, 1994). The manner in which language and mathematics are taught in the early grades leads children to separate their concepts of words and numbers. Referring to students' ability to link the two areas, Fortescue (1994) writes: "[T]he children in this class had a preconceived meaning of math—numbers and number equations independent of oral and written problem solving. This idea made the transition to communicating about math a difficult one" (p. 22). In the higher grades, as well, the notion that mathematics and language are distinct and opposing systems can limit students' ability to understand the world around them. As Bullock (1994) has argued, "The misconception of mathematics as a skill in numerical manipulations and its application in other areas of study as quantitative reasoning has hampered students' ability to develop scientific and philosophic reasoning skills" (p. 735).

Misunderstanding the close relation of language and mathematics also can pose unexpected problems for teachers. For example, when we administer a mathematics test with applied questions (or word problems), are we measuring mathematical ability or reading and comprehension? In recent years, educational psychologists have used more sophisticated techniques to measure latent traits in the results of standardized tests. Difficulty with reading and comprehension can now, to some degree, be factored out when a student's mathematical ability is measured. Ultimately, however, such a distinction between the two orders of knowledge must be recognized as artificial. As Miller (1993) has noted, "Students' understanding of mathematics is dependent on their knowledge of both mathematics as a language and the language used to teach mathematics" (p. 311). For teachers of language and mathematics, the links between words and numbers are complex, but they cannot be overlooked.

Are Language and Mathematics Separated in the Real World?

Language and mathematics are not as separated in the real world as they are in education. There are reasons why we dissect education into subjects and subdivide those subjects further into even smaller topics. For example, when a student begins music lessons, the teacher instructs the student in theory (how music works and fits together), in physical aspects (finger placement for a particular instrument), and in the emotional content of music. However, when the student plays a song, these areas are not separated. Similarly, solving problems in many areas of life involves judicious use of both words and numbers.

Experience has led us to believe that the majority of difficulties in understanding how to manipulate quantitative data stem not from the lack of memorized skills necessary to calculate formulas, but from difficulties of language. Certainly, knowing the rudiments of calculations, like knowing the rudiments of grammar, is necessary. However, as some mathematicians say, everything in mathematics is only addition, subtraction, multiplication, and division. It is the application of mathematics and communicating about mathematical concepts that require thinking.

Statistics in the Real World

Following are examples of the interaction of language and mathematics. Specifically, these examples are presented to provide evidence that many of the difficulties in working with quantitative data actually are conceptual and linguistic problems. First, there is an example provided by MacNeal (1994), whose book *Mathsemantics: Making Numbers Talk Sense* concerns the link between mathematics and semantics. We then provide a few examples from the field of educational research and evaluation.

One of the most pervasive problems in working with quantitative data is defining terms. For example, MacNeal, a consultant to the airline industry, presents the difficulty in understanding national statistics on air travel. Consider the changing definition of an airline passenger:

> In 1980, I was one passenger, ten passengers, eighteen passengers, thirty-six passengers, forty-two passengers, fifty-five passengers, seventy-two passengers, and ninety-four passengers. Each of these statements is true. I was one passenger in the sense that I was a person who traveled by air in that year. I was eighteen passengers in the sense that I made eighteen round trips. I was forty-two passengers in

the sense that on forty-two occasions I entered and exited the system of a different carrier. I was seventy-two passengers in the sense that on seventy-two occasions I was on board an aircraft when it took off from one place and landed at another. I was ninety-four passengers in the sense that I made ninety-four separate entrances and exits from airport terminal buildings. (MacNeal, 1994, p. 21)

The problem occurs when we confuse a term like *passenger* with *person*, instead of realizing that being a passenger defines what a person does. This defining of terms often leads to confusion in interpreting the statistical reports that are available each week in our newspapers and magazines. MacNeal continues his discussion of this issue by citing government officials' statements that "415 million passengers traveled by air in 1986," or "more than 6 billion passengers [were] screened at airport security checkpoints" (pp. 22–23). These statements often create impossible scenarios in which more passengers are reported than there are people currently living on the planet. Definitions often are mixed within the same statement; for example, a radio talk-show host made the following statements referring to cigarette smoking: "It kills more than 400,000 people a year. Three million of these are children." The confusion in such reports is not due to mathematical calculations. It is due to a lack of defining terms and time frames. These are language problems, not mathematical problems.

Education Statistics

As with statistics from the airline industry, language is fundamental to understanding education statistics. The procedure for studying school data usually includes the following operations:

- defining the problem
- asking the right question(s)

- determining the appropriate unit of analysis
- selecting appropriate variables
- properly defining the variables

The actual analysis of data often is a small part of the work; the data are fairly easy to understand. For example, if you were asked to describe an event (which often is the objective of statistical analysis), how would you do it? Most likely, you would include the time and date, the place of the event, and the activities that occurred. You also would include the number of participants involved and perhaps some demographics. However, you also probably would include the participants' backgrounds, their activities, their attitudes toward the event, and perhaps some follow-up information describing the impact of the event. This is the information that any reporter would investigate. Words or numbers alone would not adequately describe the event. With education statistics, quantitative data tell only part of the story; without the accompanying language, the data have no meaning.

Mistakes Regarding Concepts in Education Statistics

As in other fields of study, the mistakes made in the collection, maintenance, analysis, and reporting of education data often stem from misconceptions, not from the lack of skill to solve formulas. For example, the advent of computers has allowed researchers to collect and maintain data on entire populations. Still, university professors and institutional researchers insist on seeing the "inferential statistics" and demand to know the "p value," the probability of an event. Unfortunately, a particular management decision regarding an educational program too often is determined by whether or not a "statistically significant difference" is reported, even when data are available on a census and not on a sample of the target population. Other misconceptions are made when selecting a sample from a particular study. People often forget that the goal of the sampling is simply to select a group that is representative of the population.

Many people have made the statement, "Counting is not useful after kindergarten." This statement is wrong; in reality, much of what people do in the real world involves counting. It would be difficult to find an area of human endeavor in which quantitative data are not collected. We often define ourselves with quantities (such as height, weight, or salary). Like university professors desiring to see the "p value" from studies in which the entire population is available and in which no generalizations beyond a specific program are necessary, many unfortunately forget this simple concept: the goal of inferential statistics is the same as the goal of descriptive statistics in that we are attempting to "describe." The difference is that, with inferential statistics, the attempt is to describe the population based on a sample. Using inferential statistics incorrectly does not concern mathematical calculations; it is a conceptual error—an inaccurate use of language.

Mistakes Regarding Definitions in Studies of School Data

As with the earlier example from the airline industry, the definition of terms also is important in the collecting, analyzing, and reporting of education data. In the early 1990s, the Texas Education Agency (1994) defined gifted and talented students as students who showed high achievement in the following areas: (1) general ability, (2) specific ability, (3) creative ability, or (4) leadership. These criteria seem reasonable enough. However, this definition has similarities to a previous definition used by Texas that was more concrete. Previously, a student was identified as being gifted and talented if he or she excelled academically in specific subject(s) or had demonstrated musical or artistic talent. The problem is that many schools in the state report numbers according to the old definition and many report numbers according to the new definition. Although we assume that the "numbers" concern only mathematics, the reporting problems in this example clearly are linguistic.

Another example of a definition problem in education data regards a federally funded vocational program. To be in this program, a high school student takes a "coherent sequence of courses." The fact that the program was not defined clearly in its initial stages caused many coding and reporting inconsistencies. What defined a student as a participant in the program was never stated clearly, nor were terms such as a "coherent sequence of courses" defined properly. Personnel at different schools coded students differently; at some schools, one coding followed the student throughout the year. If the student took a vocational course in the first trimester, he or she would have been listed as a program participant even if the course was an elective and was the only vocational course that the student took during high school. At another school, the coding changed throughout the year. If the student did not take a vocational course during the first trimester (which was the school reporting trimester), yet took vocational program courses during the next two trimesters, the student would have been reported as not being in the program for that year. This is only one example of the definition problems that cause inaccuracies in the program's statistics.

The examples mentioned previously are only a few that have been used to illustrate the problems in working with quantitative data. There is a pattern; the problems usually concern conceptual and linguistic issues, not mathematical ones. Helping students learn to think through, and write about, such issues would greatly enhance the learning and application of mathematics, as well as help students learn the value of a precise vocabulary.

How Language Arts Teachers Can Enhance the Teaching of Mathematics

There are many specific lessons that secondary-school language teachers can use to enhance the learning of mathematical concepts. With the presentation of such lessons, many students will increase their understanding of words and numbers and the concepts that link the two. Perhaps there is no better time for such discussions than the teenage years. MacNeal (1994) referred to Hayakawa and Hayakawa's *Language in Thought and Action* as one of the influential popular books on language. Indeed, this was the first book that I (Dial) read on language, which I read during my late teens. MacNeal wrote the following passage about S.I. Hayakawa and the book:

> [H]e said that he and other teachers were still getting letters from students stating that the general semantics course they had taken two or three decades earlier was the turning point in their lives. From these considerations, Hayakawa concluded that general semantics in the teaching profession was particularly suitable for the transition from adolescence to adulthood, for the late high school into early college years, and that 30 years later some students would realize what they had gotten from the training. (p. 46)

It seems that adolescence—a time when people increase vocabulary and look for meaning in the world—is an appropriate time to study semantics. When students can see relations among variables and can understand concepts and functions of procedures in addition to manipulating formulas, they will have the ability to apply their qualitative and quantitative knowledge to everyday problems. Following is an example of how one mathematical term, *percent*, has as much to do with language as it does with math. Also, a few ways in which this term could be presented in a high school language course are outlined.

The Example of Percent

The word *percent* is an example of how a term that often is considered purely mathematical has as much to do with language as with mathematics. It should be noted that many math concepts also could serve as examples (for example, probability and related terms such as odds, chance, and combinations). Parker and Leinhardt (1995) provide the following excerpt that illustrates that the term *percent* is both mathematical and linguistic.

> Percent bridges two worlds. On one hand, it is a part of the mathematical ideas encompassed by multiplicative structures that extend back to the abstractions of Greek geometry (the ideas of relational arithmetic such as fractions, ratios, proportions, and rates). On the other hand, it is a ubiquitous, practical topic that has deep roots in the marketplace. Percent is present in newspapers, in magazines, in the evening news, and in everyday commerce. It is also present in various forms in textbooks from middle school to college. Current emphases in mathematics education encourage students and teachers to see the connection between real mathematical problems (in the sense of problems that intrigue mathematicians) and real-world problems (in the sense of meaningful problems that arise in everyday experiences). The assumption underlying this emphasis is that real situations will both challenge students and make the mathematics that they do more meaningful and authentic. Percent suggests itself as a useful topic, then, precisely because it is commonly present in the real world and because it is a topic related to a substantial part of the middle school and early high school curriculum, namely, multiplicative structures. (p. 422)

In investigating the teaching and learning of the term *percent*, Parker and Leinhardt reviewed some of the common problems that students have with the concept. The studies the authors reviewed indicated that students often do not even recognize the percent symbol (%) and often completely ignore it. Students also confuse the percent symbol with decimal points.

Although the concept of percent may seem somewhat trivial to an adult who understands the concept, it often is a source of confusion to students who are unfamiliar with the word. Parker and Leinhardt show that percent may be thought of as a number, a quantity, a fraction or ratio, and as a statistic or function. What is the difference in these definitions? The difference is a matter of semantics, of different ways to consider the concept of percent.

Parker and Leinhardt concluded that the difficulty in learning percent is due to language. Although closely related, the multiple meanings of the term and symbol of percent, which have developed over time, lead to confusion for many students. Their recommendations for teaching the concept of percent are (1) begin teaching the concept of ratio in the early grades; (2) use modeling and visual representation; and (3) pay attention to the language and solve interpretation problems (pp. 464–465, 471).

Other Suggestions for Classroom Lessons

There are many resources available that provide lesson ideas for integrating language and mathematics. Following are a few suggestions for language teachers who wish to integrate the learning of language with the learning of mathematics and to show students the link between words and numbers.

- Examine mathematics texts and discuss the meaning of vocabulary and concepts (Monroe, 1995).
- Teach quantitative concepts in relation to real-world experiences.
- Use the proper vocabulary regarding mathematics.
- Use writing assignments to help students clarify quantitative concepts (Armes & Sullenger, 1986;

Evans, 1984; Fortescue, 1994; Winograd & Higgins, 1994).

- Collaborate with the mathematics teacher to develop cross-curriculum lessons.
- Trace the history of numbers and how our words and symbols for numbers developed. (There are many books in print that provide a comprehensive history of numbers [for example, McLeish, 1991; Menninger, 1992]. McIntosh [1994] provides an example of how word study in geometry enhances the understanding of the concepts.)

Conclusion

It is hoped that this discussion has shown that both words and numbers represent concepts and that linguistics is an integral part of understanding quantitative data. The distance between words and numbers is not as great as many teachers of language arts may have once believed.

References

Armes, R.A., & Sullenger, K. (1986). Learning science through writing. *Science and Children, 23*, 15–19.

Bracey, G.W. (1993). Is English hazardous to mathematics? *Phi Delta Kappan, 75*(4), 432–343.

Bullock, J.O. (1994). Literacy in the language of mathematics. *American Mathematical Monthly, 101*(8), 735–743.

Capps, L.R., & Pickreign, J. (1993). Language connections in mathematics: A critical part of mathematics instruction. *Arithmetic Teacher, 41*(1), 8–12.

Evans, C.S. (1984). Writing to learn in math. *Language Arts, 61*, 828–835.

Fortescue, C. (1994). Using oral and written language to increase understanding of math concepts. *Language Arts, 71*(8), 576–580.

Hayakawa, S.I., & Hayakawa, A.R. (1989). *Language in thought and action.* Fort Worth, TX: Harcourt Brace.

Holden, C. (1993). Language may give Chinese an edge in math. *Science, 262*(5134), 651.

MacNeal, E. (1994). *Mathsemantics: Making numbers talk sense.* New York: Viking.

Maida, P. (1995). Reading and note-taking prior to instruction. *Mathematics Teacher, 88*(6), 470–473.

May, L. (1995). Speaking of math. *Teaching PreK–8, 26*(3), 24–25.

McIntosh, M.E. (1994). Word roots in geometry. *Mathematics Teacher, 87*(7), 510–515.

McLeish, J. (1991). *Number: The history of numbers and how they shape our lives.* New York: Fawcett Columbine.

Menninger, K. (1992). *Number words and number symbols: A cultural history of numbers.* New York: Dover.

Mestel, R. (1994). Languages that help children to learn math. *New Scientist, 141*(1915), 9.

Miller, K.F., Smith, C.M., & Jianjun, Z. (1995). Preschool origins of cross-national differences in mathematical competence: The role of number-naming systems. *Psychological Science, 6*(1), 56–60.

Miller, L.D. (1993). Making the connection with language. *Arithmetic Teacher, 40*(6), 311–316.

Monroe, E.E. (1995). Vocabulary considerations for teaching mathematics. *Childhood Education, 72*(2), 80–83.

Parker, M., & Leinhardt, G. (1995). Percent: A privileged proportion. *Review of Educational Research, 65*(4), 421–481.

Parker, S. (1995, October 6). Signs and symbols. *Times Educational Supplement.* 6 (4136).

Stauffer, R.G. (1966). A vocabulary study comparing reading, arithmetic, health, and science texts. *The Reading Teacher, 20,* 141–147.

Texas Education Agency. (1994). *Data standards for school district data delivery.* Austin, TX: Author.

Tracy, D.M. (1994). Using mathematical language to enhance mathematical conceptualization. *Childhood Education, 70*(4), 221–224.

Winograd, K., & Higgins, K.M. (1994). Writing, reading, and talking mathematics: One interdisciplinary possibility. *The Reading Teacher, 48*(4), 310–318.

CHAPTER 7

The Invisible Discrepancies in the Teaching of Language

KYOKO SATO

Learning to speak one's own language is both natural and instinctive according to some language theorists like Chomsky and Pinker. However, learning about the grammar(s) of the English language can be a difficult task, and *teaching* a descriptive grammar that involves the structure and meaning of English can be even more difficult. In my observations of student teachers whom I supervise, I have noticed that they possess a sophisticated intellectual knowledge about the English language, but this information is distinct and separate from knowledge of the structure of English and ways to teach it. These student teachers know *about* the English language, but they really do not know how to teach the *structure* of the language. They can conceptualize language and the various meanings of grammar with broad and accurate definitions, but when teaching they tend to reduce syntax to the questionable practice of remedying isolated sentences day after day. Furthermore, the sentence samples are not taken from the students' own writing, but usually are taken from a skills textbook, which makes the correction of errors even more remote. There rarely is a cohesive pattern or principle that evolves from the many distinct pieces of repairwork.

This chapter will address the possible reasons for the subtle shift that occurs among the student teachers' ample background knowledge, their preparation for teaching, and then their actual behavior when teaching a class—what I call the *invisible discrepancies* of teaching language. Most student teachers today are young enough to have been exposed to major reforms in English teaching. They could have learned the reader response theory of literature and the stages of the writing process during their own elementary school education. I thought the student teachers with whom I worked might have learned that there is no single reading of a work of literature, no magical format for organizing a composition, and no single correct way to write a sentence. However, in spite of the advent of new and engaging methods of reading literature and writing drafts, these student teachers in our credential program, according to my research, have not benefited from the innovative trends. In fact, 70% come from elementary school backgrounds in English seemingly untouched by these major changes.

The Three Invisible Discrepancies

The First Invisible Discrepancy

On the surface, our current student teachers look well prepared to teach, but they belie their credentials. They have taken the right courses and they say the right things in class and seminar, but when the opportunity arises to teach language and grammar, our teacher candidates revert to the way they were taught in grade school—a very traditional mode of teaching prescriptive grammar. I have read about this tendency of regression in other more general studies, but it was alarming to witness the pattern evolve in my own research.

Even though a language lesson could grow exciting and interesting simply because the meanings are ambiguous, beginning teachers typically hesitate to pursue the ambiguities. Instead, student teachers follow the routine of correcting sentences and reciting rules. My theory is that beginning teachers probably know more than they think they know; yet, instead of trusting their intuitive knowledge, they panic and shift subtly to becoming the "arbiters of correctness." For example, Deena taught a unit on autobiographies and then showed the students how to write their own life stories as a follow-up. But in her daily lesson on mechanics, she gave a disembodied exercise on how and when to use quotation marks in dialogue, yet failed to connect this useful set of punctuation cues to the students' autobiographies. You might assume that this student teacher is not skilled, but her inability to relate language study meaningfully to the students' context is more the norm than an aberration. Unfortunately, most student teachers bypass wonderful opportunities to study language that present themselves in class and are apparent to me.

The Second Invisible Discrepancy

This discrepancy in coping with the complexities in teaching language manifests itself in an avoidance relationship with the subject. During an average week, the majority of student teachers say they spend from 75% to 95% of their lessons on literature and composition. To cloak their fears of confronting language tasks such as sentence fragments and subject-verb agreement, in the name of a literature-based curriculum many student teachers take shelter in reading works and simply ignore mechanics and grammar altogether. The following is a confession from one student teacher:

> I focus on literary analysis, appreciation, and composition. Currently my students are focusing on imagery and chronological organization in their written prose. I focus on these two aspects of language study because they are my strengths. Naturally I avoid mechanics/grammar because it is my weakness. Yes, I feel that grammar is important but, frankly, the idea of getting too involved in the teaching of grammar scares me because I never know when I'm going to face a question that I simply cannot answer.

As Christenbury (1996) advises, "if you are starting...with little or no knowledge of traditional grammar, you will be handicapped in your teaching and discussion" (p. 172). After studying the student teachers' backgrounds, I found that they did have very traditional grammar instruction in elementary school and had more heavy instruction in middle school. However, there did not seem to be a successful mastery and carryover of the content.

The Third Invisible Discrepancy

The third invisible discrepancy involving the issue of standard English is the most difficult and sensitive to address. How does one teach standard English yet honor the students' diverse backgrounds? Perhaps the growing multicultural, multilingual population in southern California, USA, forces our student teachers to emphasize standard usage and discrete bits of grammar rather than allowing the students to grow into English over a longer adjustment period. The large numbers of second-language English learners who are gradually reassigned into the regular programs still speak with pronounced accents and make discernible writing errors. The teacher candidates probably feel an urgency to straighten the wrongs of these nonstandard sentences. In these situations, the student teachers need considerable help and experience in deciding what to emphasize and what to overlook, because they are confused about how to correct compositions. Intellectually, the student teachers know they should refrain from marking the students' papers filled with surface errors. However, in practice, they feel considerable pressure to usher their students quickly toward the requisite assessments necessary for redesignation out of the English as a Second Language (ESL) program. In the Los Angeles Unified School District these assessments include an oral fluency exam that is administered individually, passing reading comprehension on a standardized test at the 36th percentile, and passing a language and writing sample on the Language Assessment Scales, a standardized norm-referenced test.

The Study

For the past 4 years, I have surveyed 41 English majors at California State University, Northridge. Twenty-four were practicing student teachers, 12 were enrolled in my English methods class, and 5 are current master teachers who train student teachers in our cooperating secondary schools. I distributed a survey (see Figure on p. 130), and I followed with informal oral interviews. Because of the qualitative nature of the survey and the open-ended written responses, the results are both lengthy and unwieldy, but also are fascinating and complex. I regret not asking certain questions, but I feel that based on the information I gathered and distilled, I was able to compile a clear summary of the major findings: the invisible discrepancies between the student teachers' preparation and their actual teaching practices. Although I asked nine questions, I focus primarily on three for this chapter because they were the most relevant to my inquiry and they provoked the most complete, interesting, and powerful responses.

1. In order to determine their background knowledge of language learning, I traced the student teachers'

FIGURE: A Language Survey or "What I Wish I Had Learned About the Teaching of Language Before Student Teaching"

Instructions
Please answer each of the following questions on a separate sheet of paper. I would like to collect them and discuss your responses at your next seminar session.

1. How were you taught about language in your high school? Middle school or junior high school? Elementary level? At which grade levels? Simply recall as best as you can your experiences as a student and describe them in detail.

2. Describe your coursework preparation in language study at the university level. Was it effective? How so? If deficient, in what areas? What do English teachers need to know about the teaching of language *before* student teaching? Are there gaps that need to be filled? If so, what are they?

3. Who were the successful role models who you feel exemplified competence in the knowledge of language? Were they teachers? Parents? Ministers? If so, where? When? Why did you select them?

4. How do you define language?

5. As a student teacher, how and where in the curriculum do you teach language? Within a week's span, what percentage of time do you devote to literature? Composition? Language study? Do you think specific focus on language skills should occupy less time during the school period? More? Please elaborate.

6. What do you like best about teaching a language lesson? What do you like least? Although we try to include language study within the context of literature and composition, sometimes English teachers conduct a minilesson that focuses on a particular skill in order to review a concept like subject-verb agreement. How would you approach such a lesson, if at all? Please explain.

(continued)

FIGURE: A Language Survey or "What I Wish I Had Learned About the Teaching of Language Before Student Teaching" (continued)

7. What types of resources, for example textbooks, kits, and guidelines, are available to you? Do you use them? If so, which ones and why? If not, why not?

8. In the local southern California area, the student population is so diverse. Do you acknowledge your students' linguistic and cultural diversity? If so, how? Do you also try to prepare them for standard English and the demands appropriate for mainstream jobs and communication survival skills. How?

9. Focusing just on language study, identify what you feel are the major problems or issues in the teaching of language. If you could change any part of your background or the existing English curriculum in any way you wanted, what would you change, if anything?

10. What else should I know about language study that I have not already asked? What important questions have I overlooked that I should have included?

recollections of how they were taught language in elementary school and their attitudes now.

2. I canvassed their preparatory coursework in language study at the university and their feelings about the efficacy of these courses.

3. I polled their views on the complex issue of teaching standard English to a multilingual student population while acknowledging the uniqueness of their diversity.

What I failed to ask is their background in learning a foreign language. This information would have informed me on how

well they learned the grammar of the English language by
learning a foreign language.

The Problem

It is Christenbury's (1996) belief that "Most people
who are prepared to teach English language arts do not have
a strong language background although, clearly, language is at
the heart of our business" (p. 153). She also considers those
who have had courses in the history of the English language,
in applied linguistics, or in comparative grammar to be
among the "lucky minority." At California State University,
Northridge, the university's English credential preparation
candidates are required to take a minimum of two linguistics
courses, one in applied linguistics and the other typically in
a composition course for teachers. But if these teachers are
considered the "lucky minority," why do most of them teach
language so unimaginatively? Rouse (1967) gives the following example of an unimaginative classroom:

> Here is a typical classroom scene: the teacher is at the
> board...with a poorly wrought sentence spread out for dis-
> play like a limp mackerel, and [s]he is asking to be told
> what's wrong with it. Some boy...might say it's wrong
> because it doesn't make sense. He's right, but that is not
> what the teacher wants to hear. The correct answer is that
> the sentence has a misplaced modifier. Or suppose the stu-
> dent says a sentence just doesn't sound right. That isn't the
> correct answer either. This time he learns the sentence is
> bad because it violates parallel structure. This kind of
> thing not only happens in English classrooms, it is the
> standard practice. (p. 18)

Although this scene was described sometime in the
1960s, it is the standard among the student teachers I observe
today. The class period usually begins with "sentence repair
time" when the entire class is directed to copy a sentence

projected from an overhead projector or written on a gleaming white chalkless marker board. The teaching medium has been modernized but the routine is the same—to search for errors in a muddled, incorrect sentence. The problem with the approach is that the majority of the students do not care. While one student goes to the overhead projector and begins to erase words, rearrange parts, and insert corrections, the rest of the class usually completes unfinished homework, stares into space, or socializes until he or she finishes. After several scattered minutes, some of the students crane their necks to copy the results, but they still remain indifferent about how these changes connect to their own writing.

The Problem Is Not Just Here

The practice of teaching sentence repair unrelated to any actual composition is happening with many other classes and on a much broader and more pervasive scale than with the student teachers whom I supervise. In 1993, the National Council of Teachers of English (NCTE) Commission on Language deplored the "discrete teaching of grammar alarmingly accepted as good practice" (p. 11). Among its issues and trends for the same year, the Commission also cited the "urgent need to improve the required language study component of education for language arts practitioners at all levels" (p. 11).

Recollections of Learning About Language

To trace the history of the belief system that has such a hold on student teachers, I asked the following background questions in my survey to determine what language learning took place in their formative years of schooling:

> How were you taught about language in your own high school? Middle or junior high school? Elementary level? Simply recall as best as you can your experiences as a student and describe them in detail.

Seventy percent of the respondents remembered language as being equated with traditional grammar from elementary school through senior high school, but the bulk of the respondents remembered "straight grammar" taught the most at the middle school level. One student teacher recalled the experience succinctly, "Middle school—diagramming sentences. Yuk!"

The teacher candidates defined grammar as "old-fashioned," and their memories were overwhelmingly negative when associated with error correction. They remembered specific tasks that involved repetitive spelling and grammar drills and exercises that required copying, underlining, filling in, circling for review, and diagramming. For example, if "a lot" was written as "alot," the student was asked to write the correct version 25 times.

These rote exercises with prescribed rules always were presided over by the teacher. Written compositions especially were expected to meet a "correct" standard judged by the teacher only. The students always were aware of the presence of the teacher with a red pen poised to mark the mistakes. In fact, to this day, one student, Suzanne, carries over the intimidating mindset that language is "...always supposed to be some really proper form that I could never get right." Much to my surprise, not one student teacher remembered being taught the writing process, submitting unmarked rough drafts, or assembling student portfolios.

Other standard practices included spelling dictation tests and weekly vocabulary lists to be memorized and defined from the dictionary—vocabulary words assigned without any connection to the literature studied or to the student. Keith, who began the semester giving these kinds of vocabulary assignments himself, now admits that "words assigned like that seem to go in and out quickly with myself and my students." Keith now recognizes that drills might be detrimental and that "language is learned best when you don't even realize it. One day you use words or forms that you never used before."

In the area of oral language, the same teacher-centered mode prevailed; the teacher always talked, and the students always listened and took notes. The students were treated like receptacles and did not have a chance to take risks or to practice language.

Only 1 respondent out of 41 liked the study of language structure through traditional grammar and the diagramming of sentences, and she was one of the master teachers. Karen thought drawing the structure of a sentence was "kind of neat"; however, she came from a home environment that nurtured language and the love of reading. She and her mother visited their neighborhood public library every 2 weeks throughout her elementary school years, and this background in reading set a positive example toward language study in general, even sentence diagramming.

There were three respondents who learned grammar through the "drill and kill" method typically conducted by the teacher who fires questions at targeted students in rapid-fire succession. Although these respondents had mixed feelings about this style of teaching when they were students, they now wish they had been taught more grammar. The first is Celeste, who was accelerated into "faster" comprehension groups during her early years at a Catholic elementary school because of the competence she demonstrated in reading and writing skills. Celeste now regrets not having had more time devoted to grammar. In contrast, Tatiana resented all her early years of language study spent on boring and repetitive grammar exercises, but now bemoans the fact that "it is never 'useless' to review even simple grammar." Charlene, an older returning university student, looks back with fondness on the "formality" with which English was taught and revered in her day. She wants to preserve English as a part of our American culture, because she feels, "when a society los-es its language, it will lose itself." This opinion becomes more overt in a number of the student teachers, particularly when they encounter the diverse cultural and linguistic differences among their students.

Although the regrets about not having had enough language in the early years number only 3 out of 41 on my survey, the viewpoint expressed is very important because it underscores the "invisible" desire of the other 90% to possess a stronger foundation in grammar. The majority of the student teachers whom I supervise today feel insecure in what they do not know about the basic functions of language. They have a nagging feeling that their knowledge and understanding of grammar is weak and they need to "catch up." This feeling follows them to the classroom as they teach, and then fear can take over. They seem to remember the worst parts of teaching error correction and never fit this teaching into any larger framework.

I am reminded of a presentation that Lee S. Shulman and his team of research associates made through interactive video to our university in 1987. Shulman recounted the case study of a student teacher named Colleen:

> When teaching a piece of literature,...[she] performed in a highly interactive manner, drawing out student ideas about a phrase or line, accepting multiple competing interpretations as long as the student could offer a defense of the construction by reference to the text itself. Student participation was active and hearty in these sessions.
>
> Several weeks later, however, we observed Colleen teaching a unit on grammar. Although she had completed two university degrees in English, Colleen had received almost no preparation in prescriptive grammar.
>
> Colleen looked like a different teacher during that lesson. Her interactive style evaporated. In its place was a highly didactic, teacher-directed, swiftly paced combination of lecture and tightly controlled recitation. She was uncertain about the content and adapted her instructional

style to allay her anxiety...[thereby] limiting the range of possible deviations from the path she had designed.

I often see the same stiffness take over the student teachers whom I supervise when they teach syntax-related lessons in the classroom.

Not all the responses were negative in recounting the early years of learning about English syntax. Eleven of the respondents, or 27%, learned language through "new concepts." These oral and written activities can be expected in any balanced curriculum, but to these student-teacher respondents, the models were labeled as "innovative" and "experimental." Examples of oral communication involved tenth-grade speech and eleventh-grade debate; reading literature aloud, reciting poetry, and presenting stories orally; performing plays; and reciting famous Shakespearean speeches. Three student teachers remembered creative writing, and one in particular recalled exploring the writing of poetry and discovering that it "wasn't that hard." Two others learned language by reading the classics, and one even studied the history of the English language in senior high school.

Although only five master teachers responded, I did note a consistency among them. They all seemed to value the teaching of English syntax as a system, focusing student writing on the rhetoric of composition, and maintaining high standards. Perhaps the master teachers learned the fundamentals of language and read extensively, and as a result, they savor the written word more than the student teachers. Maybe the master teachers' opinions are a function of their maturity or the amount of their teaching experience in comparison to the student teachers'; the master teachers averaged 12 years in the classroom.

All the respondents, whether steeped in a "traditional" or "experimental" mode, agreed that reading and writing acted as the greatest catalyst toward language learning.

Background in Coursework at the University

After entering a university, prospective teachers typically learn sophisticated definitions of language that perhaps could replace their traditional mindset. The two linguistics classes required at California State University, Northridge, are somewhat helpful in widening the teacher candidates' scope of language study, but ultimately these courses are cosmetic at best in changing their belief system and behavior as student teachers. When it comes time to teach that portion of English called language study, the invisible lapse into the comfort of the belief system becomes evident.

Thirty-three percent of the respondents found university coursework in linguistics, often referred to as "the grammar requirement," as "useless" and "unrewarding." Perhaps because these classes stimulated their memories of the rather narrow, traditional emphasis in their own early schooling, these future English teachers resented the linguistics requirement from the outset. They found one class in particular, the basic grammar course, "irrelevant," "confusing," "too theoretical," "too abstract," and a "repetition of grammar learned in high school." One student teacher almost failed the course and now carries a feeling of contempt for the professor and a general dislike for the subject of grammar.

Two respondents who later became master teachers said they had to learn grammar *during* student teaching, not before, and on the job, *after* receiving the credential. Yet, whether the student teachers criticize the lack of preparation or the irrelevance of the university coursework, their teaching behavior is the same. What I most often observe in classrooms is a heavy reliance on isolated bits of traditional grammar without any study of a coherent language structure. I concluded that the disembodied and rote forms of teaching resulted from a carryover of the way student teachers were taught in their own formative schooling. I also questioned

whether the linguistics requirement at the university rein-
forced their tendency to regress. In other words, once on
their own and in front of the class, they may subconsciously
think, "I can't recall any useful, practical language strategies
from the linguistics classes so I might as well teach the way I
was taught. I learned some things from the old way, so it
should be good enough for the kids that I teach."

If the teacher candidates view the introductory grammar course at the university as being useless, unrewarding,
and irrelevant to teaching language, I questioned what they
wanted in its place. To improve their university coursework
in language education, seven English credential candidates
would like more language classes but not theory by itself.
They want it embellished within a context—like the context
of expository writing. Six more student teachers want ideas
and suggestions on how to teach language rather than learning grammar for grammar's sake, simple concepts understandable to students of middle school. Another seven student teachers are sensitive to the diverse backgrounds of their
students and would like to learn more about language differences, dialects, ESL coursework, language acquisition, and
language comparison or structure through a study of foreign
languages. Two student teachers want to know more about
the history of language and its constant evolution, particularly in the area of language variation, change, standards, and
slang.

Finally, I questioned just how much of linguistics a
preservice teacher needs to know. Weaver (1979) thinks English teachers should know the structure and the various parts
of language, an idea she expresses in the following comment:

> It may be desirable or even necessary to use some gram-
> matical concepts and terminology in helping students be-
> come more effective language users. Thus the *teacher* needs
> a fairly solid background in grammar in order to work with
> students. (pp. 89–90)

Language Diversity and Standard English

Over one third of the student teachers see their role as gatekeepers who prepare students for "good" English. These 15 respondents feel the need for students to be competent on standardized tests in school and to communicate in standard English in order to achieve vocational success. Here are some of their strong convictions:

> It is my job to prepare them for mainstream testing and jobs.

> For *practical* reasons they need to know how to speak and write Standard English. If they want career success, chances are they will be partly evaluated on their skills in this area. It's a good thing to tell students about the reality of more and more job applications asking you to "write a paragraph about yourself." I have a big poster in my room that says, "Be proud of your culture!" At the same time, I need to let them know that we live in America, and we have to deal with reality as it is.

> I...stress...the importance of real life communication skills. We just complet[ed] a real life McDonald's application and business letter containing an autobiographical paragraph and "five reasons why I'm the best person for the job" paragraph. I emphasize the need for them to market themselves.

> Allowing students to use nonstandard English in written prose does them a huge disservice. Nonstandard English is never acceptable in written expression in the mainstream community and should not be condoned in a student's *formal* writing.

> This is a philosophical problem for me and I haven't reached a conclusion. Do we do students a disservice by avoiding boring tasks like grammar? Are we so accommodating to diversity and ethnic background that we neglect to adequately teach all students to write and speak so that they can have a chance to compete in a white-collar

world? The hard realities of business do not seem to be a factor in some educational circles.

In spite of all the recent emphasis on "political correctness," the fact remains that English *is* the official language of this country, and no one knows this better than someone who does not speak English. To ignore this fact for purely ideological reasons is, in my opinion, foolish. [This last opinion is from a credential candidate who was a second-language learner.]

The student teachers make a clear distinction between oral work and written work. Although they might tolerate nonstandard dialects when students speak in class or write to fulfill freewriting and informal journal entries, the credential candidates are stringent in their expectations of standard English when students write expository compositions. (One teacher even tries to link writing exercises to standard English and morals.) This consistent underlying tone of the 15 respondents regarding standard English reveals the *third invisible discrepancy*, which exposes some subtle but real attitudes toward ethnicity. Although they might recognize varied accents and nonstandard usage patterns in speech—in writing, they slam the door shut on diversity.

In one methods class session, when the discussion turned to African American Vernacular English, the talk suddenly escalated into a rather heated debate over what "level" of language to permit. Although some students had learned from their university linguistics courses that black English follows a consistent system, others never knew that it was considered a language; they always considered it street slang and never would permit it in written work. Wolfram (1993) would call this latter judgment of African American Vernacular English "grammatically correct but socially incorrect" (see Chapter 5 by Wolfram for further discussion of Vernacular English). "Who's ever going to accept someone for a job who says, 'I be qualified'?" shouted one woman who represented many students in the class. Opposing students responded that English teachers have to be sensitive to dialects because of the risk of alienating the students. We ended our discussion because of time constraints, but I have been continuing the incomplete strands of dialogue in my mind ever since. The deeply rooted attitudes and feelings provoked by language learning and diversity were so potent in that class session because they lay so deeply buried. The following comments represent the unanimity student teachers feel about written language:

> Written and oral communication are vastly different. Competition in this country is fierce. Thus, a student must know the American way of the world through written communication. Meanwhile, oral language and cultural diversities can be preserved.

> I teach a section on the differences between standard and nonstandard English and the appropriateness of both. Basically I tell them they can speak any way they wish as long as they are willing to pay the consequences. Certain areas, business, politics, education, etc. demand a standard level of communication—that is standard English. Since I also coach football and track, I use the example that when I am coaching I don't necessarily use standard English all of the time, but I do inside the classroom and with my peers.

> Creative writing...let it rip! Be you. Dialect goes in my classes. [But] I insist all kids write standard for composition. I try to talk to them about what it's like "out there." They don't realize it's [writing in nonstandard English] a big "no no."

Interestingly only 1 student teacher out of 41 redefined standard English not as a monolith but as a somewhat varied dialect in and of itself, depending on who speaks it. She also was the only student teacher who would teach standard English not because of her personal mission but because she is conceding to the parents' wishes. Parents want what is best for their children's success via "proper" language, whether it is defined within the parameters of the "English only" movement or learning what parents interpret to be standard English. Some Spanish-speaking parents want their children to learn to speak English early in life, resulting in a boycott staged in a poor, industrial section of Los Angeles, California. A number of Latino parents want to have the option to put their children into an "English only" program (*Los Angeles Times*, p. B11). The same student teacher who would teach standard English to accede to parents' wishes admits the following:

> This is quite a problem. I would warn kids of the language prejudice out there that might keep them from climbing up, but it would be hard to teach standard English, or rather, *my* English, or the English of a newsperson. This has much to do with identity and cultural/political issues which I find troubling. But parents do seem to want their kids to be taught this way—to succeed this way.

In a geographic and culturally opposite part of the United States, Dodd (1996) surveyed 25 parents in southern Maine. The parental position was similar in wanting the "basics" for their children and ultimately desiring the "correct" language that would ensure their well-being in society. She summarizes the parents' attitude in the following excerpt:

> The parents I interviewed all wanted their children to write and speak correctly, and many believed that the study of grammar was very important in this regard.... Many of them had little or no understanding of the process approach to teaching writing.... One reason for a parent's tendency to prefer traditional practices is that long-held beliefs are not easily changed. (pp. 58–59)

Implications for English Teachers

What can we learn from these community feelings toward standard English? Student teachers still mark the surface errors on their students' papers first, especially the written work of limited English proficient (LEP) students, the very population for whom syntactical rules should come last. Instead of using a rubric and evaluating the work by the criteria agreed on, there is an overwhelming amount of effort expended toward error hunting. Writing a single overall comment at the end of a composition is still rare among my student teachers.

However, in contrast to the 15 respondents who insist on teaching standard English and who probably would emphasize syntactic rules, there was another small but committed group of six student teachers who would honor fluidity in language first, even the primary dialect language if necessary, because they feel it is critical to the students' self-esteem. In other words, they would allow conversations in the native tongue as well as organizing compositions in the primary language. As skills improve, writing in English and the grammar and structure would follow. They feel that language fluency is the first priority for an attitudinal reason: receptivity toward the new language would be far more positive if the nonnative students were comfortable in using their primary language first. Assignments would be informal, and writing would consist of freewrites or personal narratives that could include slang and dialect. One student teacher would graduate the writing assignments, beginning with freer composition forms at first, such as journals. Then as students began to like the writing process, she would follow with more traditional assignments, like a business letter, to acquaint the students with societal demands in written English.

When oral skills are encouraged, these six teachers would allow students to speak often, just to build confidence.

And they would encourage their class to speak without fear of correction. Without the feeling of intimidation, these teachers hope, the LEP student will grow to a new consciousness of how language works. The following are comments from two teachers:

> I will encourage second-language students to speak the language often, listen to the sounds closely, read and write without feeling intimidated by the class. We all make mistakes! We need to view mistakes as a way to grow and raise our conscious awareness to a new level. *Mistakes are good!*

> The other day I said, "boughten" (oops!) but if you think about English language rules, it makes sense! We say, "throw and thrown, bite and bitten, write and written. When students can see that their mistakes are not "dumb," but rather an extension of their knowledge, it makes those usage rules easier to swallow.

If more teachers like the ones above were to create an atmosphere in which their students could feel comfortable making mistakes, it would be easier to show patterns of sentence construction rather than discrete error corrections.

From the perspective of two foreign-born credential candidates who were themselves ESL students, each revealed that "old-fashioned" grammar had a minimal impact on their acquisition of English. Richard, a student teacher from Armenia, felt that the study of grammar was too abstract to have any lasting value. Jolene, a first-generation immigrant student from Korea, felt that writing and reading seemed more important than any emphasis on grammar. She said that she learned to speak the language through aural modeling and by listening to the teacher and mimicking, repeating, and copying the way he or she spoke.

To teach standard English while honoring students' diversity is an enormously complex and sensitive task. Standard English as a socializing influence is viewed as being very important by many parents. Some student teachers argue that a single standard English language exists and simply want to know how to teach it; others contend that "standard" English is indefinable. The latter group feels that language, spoken or written, is more the students' responsibility. They think that if we as teachers want to further language awareness, we should assign activities integrated into the students' own reading and writing; thus, the students will learn language naturally through exposure and practice. In contrast, the former group maintains that language, or more specifically standard English syntax, should be taught directly.

The problems that accompany the increasing heterogeneity in our classrooms emerge frequently enough. Compounding the challenges of heterogeneity is the growing diversity of our student population. If teachers view the ESL learner as an intruder and a contributing factor to the already declining literacy levels, the teaching task will become burdensome and frustrating.

Teachers can take the first step toward bridging the initial gap between the linguistic isolation experienced by the LEP students and the gradual fluency they could acquire by accepting the levels of language acquisition and dialects as nonjudgmentally as possible. Teachers who realize that dialect is an integral part of the learner can then progress to create a meaningful context for the language minority student. From this point the instructor can guide the student toward a perceived standard dialect by teaching a *descriptive* grammar rather than a *prescriptive* one (see Chapter 5 for a detailed discussion of descriptive and prescriptive grammar).

Student teachers are part of a generation that still was taught the basics of English grammar traditionally, rigorously, and unevenly. To overcome this background, they often lapse into a pattern in which they teach correctness. In so doing they are not aware of how well their students, including ESL students, already know language. If only our student teachers could remember that the students already know a language and that knowledge can transfer over to the acquisition of English.

Conclusions

I conclude this chapter by offering some suggestions for change and reform in order to reduce the invisible gaps typically experienced by the precredential teaching candidates *after* they enter the classroom.

- There is a need for a major overhaul of the teaching of language at each level—elementary, secondary, and postsecondary—beginning with the elementary school language arts preparation program. The precredential coursework designed for elementary school teachers should include a strong exploratory language component on what English is, what grammar is, and how language works, especially in the context of writing. Student teachers also should be exposed to the variations of English dialect. Otherwise, elementary and secondary teachers will continue to perpetuate the cycle of teaching English language skills as drills and have an almost irreversible effect on yet another generation of prospective teachers.

- The required coursework in grammar at the university can be changed either by incorporating a contiguous practicum strand or by adding a laboratory section. This would be an opportunity to flesh out rather complex linguistic theories and to internalize them before student teaching. Credential candidates could use the extended time in mock sessions, practicing how to apply and teach some of the facets of syntax, morphology, or phonology that they previously have only memorized. For example, if actual sample student papers were distributed and preservice candidates had the chance to compare among themselves what syntax to accept and how to comment on these aspects of composition, perhaps some of the confusion that occurs during practice teaching could be alleviated. The Methods of Teaching English class, typically in the College of Education, devotes at least 12 hours to the writing process and to some composition teaching techniques. The class also addresses specific language issues, such as how to respond to students' sentences with the most simple and clear suggestions for revision. However, this course is limited to one semester, which leaves other equally important strategies to address.

- Perhaps if the professors of the required university grammar course were familiarized with the *Reading and Writing Content Standards for Kindergarten Through 12th Grade* (1997), they could teach the theories and applications of their linguistics courses, maintaining an awareness of the general language arts guidelines followed by public schools.

- In addition, if university linguistics professors could evaluate the grammar textbooks that are available in the public secondary schools, then the instructors might teach the linguistic theories within the realistic parameters of what is available—and what is not—to the student teachers. The following comment is from a practicing second-semester student teacher:

> The biggest problem that I found with grammar books is that they can't explain things well enough to get the kids to say, "I understand what they want me to do now." Last semester...I asked

them [the students] to go home and read something.... When we read it the next day in class together, I noticed that it was going 12 feet over the head of every single student in that room. And it was going 12 feet over my head. I just looked at them and asked, "So who understands what we just read?" Everybody just sat there. That's the problem with most grammar books. They just cannot explain things in plain English. They go into these long convoluted explanations of everything so all meaning is lost.

- The most complex suggestion for change involves the preparation of preservice teachers (K–12) to include a broadened dimension of language study. The issues of second-language learners, diversity, and standard English are difficult to address because they include a personal attitude and bias instead of a dispassionate understanding of multilingual students' needs. Trying to change language attitudes after student teachers are hired is even more difficult. I have participated and led staff inservice meetings, which typically are held after school in uncomfortable settings. Any topic inviting teachers to embrace change and diversity, be it the learning handicapped, issues of gender bias, or English competency and standards, usually is met with minimal acceptance if not resistance.

The most important, albeit difficult suggestion for reform in the preparation of preservice teachers, K–12, calls for a pivotal change among university faculty. In their charge to prepare future teachers toward more effective English and language arts teaching, university faculty need to make the broadened dimensions of language study more meaningful. The issues of second-language learners, diversity, and standard English are controversial and particularly difficult for student teachers to address because they include a personal attitude and bias instead of a dispassionate understanding of multilingual students' needs.

As I have analyzed and reflected on my last suggestion of a broader, more impartial attitude toward language teaching, I see the enormity of the task, but the key in achieving this goal lies within the reach of the university faculty. The very nature of language is such an integral part of our identity that when the time comes to transform it for instruction, student teachers often unconsciously recall their personal belief system without even realizing it. To raise their awareness level *before* becoming student teachers, university professors might rely less on high-level linguistic abstractions and instead reveal a close and personal look at their own language biases. In turn, these personal revelations could be a powerful influence in getting preservice teachers to closely examine their personal attitudes toward language, and realize that this self-knowledge is just as critical as the acquisition of their academic linguistic knowledge base. If honest self-scrutiny were to be encouraged by professors, accompanying each phase of linguistic coursework at the university, then perhaps student teachers could expand their limited language agendas beyond the narrow parameters of the correct and the incorrect. If the academic knowledge were internalized into a personal context, then the invisible discrepancies might surface, allowing student teachers to see more clearly that English is not a narrow portion of a subject discipline to be memorized and mastered. Rather, English is a difficult, ever-changing, ambiguous, frustrating, but fascinating system of symbols to embrace, to work at, and to create.

References

Christenbury, L. (1996). *Making the journey*. White Plains, NY: Longman.

Dodd, A.W. (1996). What do parents mean when they talk about writing "basics" and what should English teachers do about it? *English Journal*, *85(1)*, 58–61.

National Council of Teachers of English Commission on Language (1993). Trends and issues in English instruction, 1993—three summaries. *Council-Grams: News and Information for Leaders of the Council, LX*(3), 11.

Parents urging English-only classes end weeklong boycott. (1996, February 22). *Los Angeles Times*, p. B11.

Rouse, J. (1967). How to manufacture tin ears. *Media and Methods*, 16–20.

Shulman, L.S. (1987). Knowledge and teaching: Foundations of the new reform. *Harvard Educational Review, 57* (1).

The Commission for the Establishment of Academic Content and Performance Standards. (1997). *Reading and writing content standards for kindergarten through 12th grade* (Draft No. 1). Sacramento, CA: Author.

Weaver, C. (1979). *Grammar for teachers: Perspectives and definitions*. Urbana, IL: National Council of Teachers of English.

Wolfram, W. (1993). Varieties of American English. In L.M. Cleary & M.D. Linn. (Eds.), *Linguistics for teachers* (pp. 103–130). New York: McGraw-Hill.

Strand Four

Emerging Trends in
Language Study

CHAPTER 8

Language Education in the 21st Century: Dreaming a Caring Future

JOHN S. MAYHER

f one looks at the future with hope, as I certainly want to do, then he or she can anticipate that the children and adolescents who now are living and learning in whole language classrooms will be a positive force for educational reform in the next century. Their definition of normal will not be the common-sense experience of learning from worksheets and basals while sitting in rows, but instead will be what is now the uncommon-sense experience of learning through meaning-making uses of language: by reading real books and writing real texts while sitting in circles and working in groups.

So, in some respects those of us who are working in rich language environments and are struggling to teach in uncommon-sense ways are doing so for the future as much as for the present. We are trying to break the cycle of stasis that has meant that the U.S. classrooms of the 1990s look a lot like the classrooms of the previous century. A time traveler from the 1890s might not recognize a lot about U.S. culture, but put him or her in most classrooms and it would all look fairly familiar. Sadly, it would look most familiar in higher education and in secondary schools, and one of the reasons school change has been so glacially slow is that "serious" academic environments remain teacher-centered domains. This continues to define "real" school as teacher-centered, and it makes student-centered language learning only suitable for very young children who still have the luxury of treating learning as fun.

The pressures on secondary teachers to teach "content" continues to encourage the atomization of reading and the English language arts. It may be less common than it used to be to divide reading, writing, vocabulary, and spelling, but too many teachers still have not used the power of integration to help students master all the language arts together. Engaging students with the texts they read and the texts they write is far easier and promotes far more long-lasting learning than the atomized approach ever has.

There are tensions at all levels, of course, so I was glad to see a report in *Education Week* in March 1994 that showed that introducing more formal and atomized approaches to literacy instruction in kindergarten actually was harmful to children's later command of reading and writing and to a whole range of other abilities including math and science. We uncommon-sense, whole language teachers have been saying this for a long time, but it always is nice to have research that shows it to be true. Such research will not have much effect, but it may provide another bit of shielding for those of us who are trying to do something different, and if that is true, we all can breathe a little easier.

The pressures to keep things the same or to return to a supposed golden age when everyone was literate are always with us, because as the culture changes we want to find our way back to the basics we hope will make everything well again. I, too, share the goal of trying to make the world better, but I do not think that path can be found by looking backward and being nostalgic.

This is true partly because the data do not support the notion of a golden age—literacy levels actually have been rising rather than falling in the 20th century, but the demands of literacy have been rising even faster, thereby creating the appearance of decline. This is true mostly because the schools of previous generations "succeeded" in large part by serving a steadily shrinking percentage of each age group from sixth grade on. Our culture no longer can support schools that do not educate everyone, and helping all students achieve excellence remains the major challenge of the next century.

From Language to Community

Other forces that are in conflict now and that will influence the future of language study are the struggle between meaningfulness and meaningfreeness, and the competing definitions of the curriculum in terms of whether it continues to be structured by partial, separate disciplines, or whether it can be redefined holistically in integrated, interdisciplinary ways. I see no happy future for language study in the 21st century unless its scope is enlarged beyond literacy education to encompass the whole process of schooling, of teaching and teacher education, and the role of the school in the larger culture.

I know that my Utopian vision will be contested strongly by many people, and I will address some of the objections I anticipate. However, any good prognosticator tries to shape as well as anticipate the future, so I will attend most directly to the schools I would like to see in the next century without being concerned about the feasibility of my dreams.

In my first set of dreams I will briefly sketch the growing nightmare I see in our schools and in our society in the

United States. The second set—the Utopian set—will provide a glimpse of the schools I would like to see.

Dystopia: Schools as Denial Agencies

As Noddings (1992) pointed out in *The Challenge to Care in Schools*, the world in which we live has changed dramatically, but the schools have changed little if at all. (See also Cuban's [1993] *How Teachers Taught* for an effective discussion of the lack of school change and some of the causes for it.) Noddings emphasized that the changes we are experiencing are most dramatic for our children. These changes range from the explosive growth of single-parent families and the spread of drugs and guns throughout the urban culture to more benign influences such as television, video games, and computers. Schools that were designed for past generations simply are not a good match for the world we live in at the end of the 20th century, and will be even less so in the 21st century.

This set of changes most powerfully affects children and adolescents who live in the inner cities of the United States, but in recent years it has become increasingly clear that even affluent suburbs are not immune from these influences. Studies show that even children who are learning to read are very rarely choosing to do so, and there are few if any suburbs that are immune from the effects of divorce and drugs, a combination that affects the affluent as well as the poor.

Parents may still want to protect their children and may still believe that their schools are "good" because they still are producing "winners" in the competitive race to get students into a selective college. But as I visit such supposedly "excellent" schools—public and private—I continue to see a common-sense classroom pattern of teacher-centered rote recitation that is producing a generation of students for whom schooling has been disconnected from learning. These future "winning students" value school only for the credentials it can provide and see no connection between their real lives and the curriculum. They arrive at college prepared for more of the same and are shocked and resentful when a college teacher challenges their expectations and actually expects them to engage with the material. Sadly, such challenging college instruction is the exception, not the rule, and too many college courses are as mindless as their secondary school predecessors.

However bad it may be in the affluent suburbs of the United States, however, it is worse in inner-city communities where police corruption and the effects of drugs are evident. Schools in such environments have lost much of their potential role as centers of hope, but I think they can once again gain it if they dramatically reconceptualize their role. I will address this role when I present my Utopia later in the chapter.

Where Does Language Study Fit in Such a Grim World?

The people who want the school to serve as a denial agency do not want much real language study at all. They are the people I referred to earlier who look for meaningfreeness as the hallmark of the literacy education process. Documented most powerfully by James Moffett (1988) in *Storm in the Mountains*, these people want the school to keep children safe from ideas by teaching them to read by using phonics strategies and by pretending consistently that texts have determinable, fixed, literal meanings. Extending beyond beginning reading and writing instruction, such people want to censor literature so that children are exposed only to happy books with middle-class nuclear families who share their religious beliefs. Moffett warns the reader that as student writing becomes genuinely a meaning-making activity and not a dummy run or an empty exercise, then it too is beginning to see the threat of censorship.

By denying the reality of the social changes that have happened since the 1940s, meaningfree people hope to protect their children from harsh realities by creating a school that somehow is an island apart from that world and not a living part of it. It is easy to understand why such denial is attractive, but I would argue that it will not work and that it has not worked, because much of what I see actually happening in the common-sense schools of our culture is consistent with the denial-based, meaningfree curriculum. The workbooks still are with us (albeit sometimes now on computers, as Smith [1986] has pointed out in *Insult to Intelligence*); controversy has been washed out of the social studies curriculum; children still are writing boring reports on the major products of countries of the world; and worst of all, we are assessing our educational progress with more and more standardized tests whose multiple choice format and mindless content drive the curriculum further and further into irrelevance.

Given the bland and too often mindless curricula that we have resorted to in an effort to avoid controversy, the change required will be deep and fundamental. Considering our history and the power of tradition, no one can be very optimistic that such changes are possible, much less likely. However, there are signs of hope in the sustained quality of the current movement for educational reform; in the growing recognition that something new is required, not just doing the same old things better; and in some powerful grass-roots movements that actually are having an effect in many, particularly elementary, classrooms and of which the whole language movement is the paradigm case.

From Common Sense to Uncommon Sense

I have written an entire book about how difficult it is to change our conceptions of school (Mayher, 1990), so I will not repeat all of the arguments here. Essentially, the problem derives from the fact that all of us teachers learned to define the notion of school through our own experience of what I call mostly "common-sense studentdom." Our sense of what teachers and students do, of what classrooms look like, and of what the rules are that govern who does what have defined a set of normal expectations that pervade our culture—hence the term *common sense*. It requires a particularly powerful act of the imagination to picture something substantially different—what I came to call *uncommon sense*. The insidious quality of educational common sense is that it is largely unconscious; it guides our perceptions but we are not aware of its effects until we try to change.

We all know that change is difficult. The tried and true is familiar and comfortable, and we are reluctant to move into new patterns of behavior and new understandings of the way things could work. So, we will need some powerful motivation in order to move in new directions. We also must consider the question: Why should we attempt such a dramatic set of changes? My answer is that the "tried" is no longer "true," that the familiar has forced us into habits that do not serve our students, our culture, or the future. Whatever virtues our school system may have had for the first half of the 20th century, the system has been increasingly under fire in the second half; by now the consensus is that dramatic changes must be made if schools are to serve the students and the society of the next century.

The issue, therefore, is not whether or not change is necessary, but rather the direction and nature of the changes that are required. I already have explained that neither a nostalgic attempt to return to the past nor a denial that the world has changed can solve the growing problems. The solution, therefore, must come some other way. For me, the particulars of the vision I espouse here are less significant than their spirit: they are rooted in a renewed commitment to the children of the United States and to a positive vision of the future. I am not so naive as to believe that positive thinking alone will solve our problems, but I do know that cynicism and bitterness surely will exacerbate them.

Even those of us who have been struggling to remove our common-sense lenses and see a new uncommon-sense world continually relapse into old patterns. But, to have an idea of where we are going, we need a vision of where we want to go. So, I now present some pleasant dreams of the kinds of schools I would like to see my granddaughters attend in the 21st century.

Utopia: Schools as Caring Learning Communities

So what would schools look like that did not deny the reality of the present and that said YES! to a holistic future? Following Noddings (1992), they will be what I will call *caring learning communities*. Our goal, in her words, is to

> produce competent, caring, loving, and lovable people...[and to recognize] that caring in every domain implies competence. When we care we accept the responsibility to work continuously on our own competence so that the recipient of our care—person, animal, object, or idea—is enhanced. There is nothing mushy about caring. It is the strong resilient backbone of human life. (pp. 174–175)

There is nothing incompatible about caring and learning. That is, some progressive educational programs have emphasized being supportive of student efforts to the extent that they neither criticized them nor pushed them toward higher achievement. Noddings's vision of caring—and mine—is quite the contrary of that; we are convinced that quality is one very important feature of caring. Such quality includes quality of work, quality of commitment to others, quality of concern for the environment, and so on. Schools do not help students by suggesting that anything goes and that excellence is not worth striving for. In my caring learning communities the message of commitment to the highest standards would be sent every day.

What would be different about my Utopian school, however, is that it would believe neither that children must be punished as a path to excellence, nor that only a few children can be expected to achieve. The connection of a harsh and punitive atmosphere with high standards is one of the most damaging of our common-sense beliefs, but even worse is our assumption that only a few children can do good work. Although extraordinary talent at the level of Mozart, Einstein, or Michael Jordan is undoubtedly rare, remarkable achievements are within the grasp of many more children and adolescents than we have recognized. One of the great achievements of whole language approaches to schooling has been to demonstrate this. My caring learning communities would not sell anyone short.

My learning community will have at least the following characteristics:

multigenerational—parents, children, and other members of the community learning and growing in the same place;

inclusive (and inviting)—places where children and adults want to be;

open almost all the time—all day, late at night, and all year;

multipurpose—a place where many social services and other community functions would be available to serve the students, staff, and community;

beautiful—the best possible physical environment, and one which all members of the community take a role in preserving and enhancing—one aspect of caring for both the natural world and the human world;

warm—where people's names are known and they are greeted with a smile;

friendly—where we explicitly learn to value others and enact the values of caring by understanding how individuals and groups can create rivals and enemies;

respectful—where we explicitly learn to value and to treat ethically those who are different from us or with whom we disagree;

safe—drug and violence free;

democratic—run by the people it serves; children and adults will work together to create structures, policies, and rules that ensure fairness and equity, peace and harmony, and that put power in the service of learning;

explicitly antiracist, antisexist, and anticlassist—whatever the actual population of the learning community and whatever else may be on the curricular agenda, a consistent curricular text and subtext will be to confront and challenge the racist, sexist, and classist mores of our culture;

consistent—a place where teachers and students stay together (by mutual consent) in the same building and in the same space within the same school for several years, and a place filled with plants, animals, and equipment that the children can learn to practice caring for;

meaning-based learning environments—for all participants: students, teachers, administrators, parents, aides, social service workers, medical personnel, and police officers. The key notions involved in being meaning based are choice (by the learner) of what he or she wants to learn in a process of negotiation among learners and teachers about how to become meaning based and how to demonstrate competency; we must give all students what all students need—genuine opportunities to explore the questions central to human life;

high quality—committed to high standards for all learners, and committed to working on them in such a way that learners who have not achieved particular competencies deemed important are regarded as not yet having done so, rather than as failures; failure is therefore something that attaches to the institution, not to the individual;

nonhierarchical—where programs for all students are equally rich and meaningful, not just for those deemed to be "college bound";

professional—where teachers and other adults are treated like competent adults, because unless they are so treated they will not treat the children and adolescents in their charge that way;

learner and learning centered—where the needs and interests of the learner in the community are the basis for curricular organization, rather than conventional disciplines, subjects, skills, or content; where negotiation is the framework within which curricular decisions are made. Whatever is still really alive about the conventional curriculum and the abilities needed to acquire and use it can be learned in such contexts, but in the Utopian school, the learning process always will be whole, never partial, and always will be contextualized, never out of context.

Human Schools for Human Beings

I could go on fantasizing about the wonders of the Utopian school. It certainly is a pleasant change to imagine school as a voluntary environment that feeds the spirit, the heart, the body, and, the mind; where all participants feel welcome and cared for; and where the business of learning and the business of living are not separate but whole.

What I think language practitioners and theorists have not yet done (and those of us concerned with secondary English and reading have done even less) is to make the human experience of living and learning in classrooms the central concern of the school. We have claimed for generations that we have had an impact on students' lives through the literature we teach, and more recently through the writing they do, but our practice in those areas too often has belied our lofty rhetoric. Our tests in literature and our responses to student texts too often have sent the message that what really counts is recall of detail or form.

Being concerned with and responding to the real issues in student lives would be a profound change for most schools and for all of us involved in them: teachers, students, parents, and administrators. Even those of us who have tried to make changes in the past decade generally have done so within a framework that essentially is transmission based: adults telling children what we think they need to know. The curriculum has been too narrowly focused, using only a fraction of our multiple intelligences (Gardner, 1983). The traditional curriculum has been linguistically and mathematically focused, and transmitted within a set of autonomous and independent disciplines. Learning has been competitively driven, based on the two assumptions of capitalism defined by social Darwinism: that there is a scarcity of talent, and that the race for success inevitably will reward the able and punish the less able.

As we learn more about learning—intelligence and multiple intelligences—about teaching, and about human growth and development, it seems more and more the case that this common-sense vision of schooling and its associated assumptions and processes are not merely false, but they actually are harmful. They are not merely harmful for the poor and others who do not fit neatly into the percentage of conforming students, but they are damaging for the so-called "best and the brightest" students as well. No one learns best in the schools we have, and all children and adolescents would learn better and grow more healthily in caring learning communities such as those I have described. The key will be the ability to work together to find a way to build these ideal schools for future generations.

References

Cuban, L. (1993). *How teachers taught: Constancy and change in American classrooms, 1890–1990*. New York: Teachers College Press.

Gardner, H. (1983). *Frames of mind: The theory of multiple intelligences*. New York: Basic Books.

Mayher, J. (1990). *Uncommon sense: Theoretical practice in language education*. Portsmouth, NH: Boynton/Cook.

Moffett, J. (1988). *Storm in the mountains*. Carbondale, IL: Southern Illinois University Press.

Noddings, N. (1992). *The challenge to care in schools*. New York: Teachers College Press.

Smith, F. (1986). *Insult to intelligence*. New York: Arbor House.

CHAPTER 9

Reading and Writing in the Shadow of Film and Television

HAROLD M. FOSTER

People have a rainbow of new information sources based on technology, including film and television and the Internet and World Wide Web. Even print media has changed as a result of technology. Contents of newspapers and magazines reflect thought processes that do not require lengthy stories with beginnings, middles, and ends. International newspapers like *USA Today* are like print televisions with facts, color, and an endless variety of short, punchy "infotainment." The delivery of print has changed because of technology. Newspapers like *The New York Times* and the *Wall Street Journal* have become global and can be delivered to your doorstep anywhere in the world. Also, now with the advent of new technology, newspapers and magazines are available instantly on the World Wide Web. Almost the entire world shares the same images—whether they are images of affection, violence, war, or any other elements of modern society. Television and film mediate these experiences for almost everyone on earth.

The model citizen at the end of the 20th century uses all the wonderful resources available. Success requires and welcomes a blend of all media and all technology. Most highly educated people take their knowledge from a blending of media sources that are difficult, if not impossible, to separate.

If standards for media are high, if communities are uplifted, if standards of living are raised, if the literacy rate is improved, then media globalization is good. However, if violence increases, if literacy rates remain low, if a sameness replaces cultural richness, then this globalization is bad. I suspect both scenarios are happening.

Raising Standards: How Films Helped Me Deal with the Holocaust

The Holocaust is an extremely important event to me because I am Jewish and I was born in the late 1940s, near the end of World War II. My earliest memories of the Holocaust were of newsreel footage of parents and children being dragged out of their homes by soldiers. I was very young when I saw this and it stuck with me. Since then I have learned about the Holocaust from many sources, including speakers, journals, magazines, newspapers, and books. I have read scholarly works like *War Against the Jews: 1933–1945* by Lucy Dawidowicz and classics like *Anne Frank: The Diary of a Young Girl*. I know concentration-camp survivors who have given me vivid first-person accounts of their experiences. I also have read many times Gerda Weissmann Klein's moving memoir, *All But My Life*.

I always have been profoundly dumbfounded by this human catastrophe, but as I turn 50 years old I feel I have come to grips with this event, aided in great part by what I consider "closure documents." Now I cope with the Holocaust in a spiritual sense, the way one mourns a parent who died many years ago. Among the Holocaust "documents" that have brought me this closure are two films: *Shoah* and *Schindler's List*. Although these films are very different, they complete my needs in different ways. The documentary *Shoah*, which is a comprehensive account by Holocaust survivors, gives me an emotional account of the horrors. But *Shoah* is a work of art, carefully structured to show the unraveling of the moral and physical world. At the end of the film a survivor of the Warsaw ghetto revolt recounts his last sight of this ghetto formerly teeming with people. He sees nothing but rubble—no life—as if he is the last living person on earth. This is a perfect emotional ending to a Holocaust work that transforms this documentary into a vehicle for emotional mourning. Although the film includes only true accounts, the accounts are shaped into a stunning and tragic artistic narrative.

On the other hand, *Schindler's List* provides me with a sense of redemption. Although every Holocaust work can be accused of being too fictional, too sentimental, or too marginal, for me *Schindler's List* was seminal. My strongest association with the film is outside the narrative framework. What I associate with most in the movie is the bittersweet music and the images of the candles at the beginning and at the end. Certain images stick in my mind: the burning bodies, the final long shot of the destruction of the ghetto, people's faces, and the snow. When the film turns from fiction to documentary at the end, the actors and survivors place stones on the real Jerusalem grave of Schindler. For the viewer, it is like a funeral—something sad, tragic, and completed.

Are these two works just movies? Perhaps. But I felt something stronger and more important, like a religious experience composed of fragments, images, music relating to a theme, and stories told brilliantly in films. I never will completely understand the Holocaust, but this important issue in my life was resolved with the aid of powerful films along with a variety of other media, including books.

What the New Media Has Done to Reading and Writing

When I wrote my book *Crossing Over: Whole Language for Secondary English Teachers*(1994), I abandoned the objective tone of a scholar. I made this decision for several reasons. For one, I did not believe that what I was saying was objective. I wanted my readers to know that these were my ideas based on research and experience, but that readers' opinions counted in an endeavor as complicated as English teaching. I felt the first-person accounts written by Nancie Atwell (*In the Middle: Writing, Reading, and Learning with Adolescents*, 1987) and Mike Rose (*Lives on the Boundary: The Struggles and Achievements of America's Underprepared*, 1989) were closer in spirit to what I had to say than work that sounded more scholarly. I was hoping this reader-friendly style would make my book more interesting. My classes constantly lamented the dull and removed nature of most texts they read, which is a sad commentary on the writings of English teachers.

However, there is another issue at work with first-person scholarship. This issue is identified clearly by Purves (1994), who made the point that the scholarly voiced essay hearkens back to a time before the electronic media. He wrote with ironic humor, "Don't tell students to be too interesting or imaginative; watch out for images and metaphors; keep personality out of it" (p. 27). Purves went on to explain how media has changed the very nature of English teaching. The following excerpt is from Purves' essay, "People Prose":

> Look back to the 1960s and see the culmination of the print approach to the teaching of the language arts. Note the jargon: *the tripod of language, literature, and composition; structuralist criticism and grammar (with its transformational modulation); reading comprehension; text-based rhetoric;*

structure and sequence; Socratic or inductive teaching; the acquisition of skills; comprehensive norm-referenced; and experimental design and linear regression models in research.

In the 1990s, different jargon dominates our view: *whole language, reader response, student empowerment, language experience, communicative competence, recursive processes, composing, discussion-centered or student-centered classrooms, portfolio assessment, and ethnographic research.* All of these terms betoken a multidimensional space, perhaps a hyperspace. It is a space dominated by images that emerge from television and the computer. (pp. 21–22)

I agree with Purves. In *Crossing Over* I described this curriculum that I believe is a holistic approach to English teaching necessitated by an electronic culture that places holistically thinking students in our classrooms. I described this curriculum for our time with my own voice and through many of my own experiences.

The voice in my writing changed because I no longer had faith in the old way, the "out of body" pretense of objectivity (no I, you, or we). I no longer had faith in the old clinical writing style either as truth telling, persuasion, or even interesting writing. I felt far more authentic adopting the conventions addressed by Purves. I am sure I wrote *Crossing Over* because of my disposition to write in the voice with which I was most comfortable, a voice influenced by reading, but also by film and television. Certain reviewers characterized *Crossing Over* as postmodern scholarship, and I accept this. I believe this book also reflects a postmodern, postindustrial viewpoint conditioned by what Real (1989) called *Super Media*: all media that "surround us and affect us with a pervasiveness impossible to avoid" (p. 14). Real wrote, "Our media, ourselves" (p. 15). Now it is the job of educators to creatively understand "our media" in order to understand the "ourselves" of students we face every day.

What Research Says About the Impact of the Media

For the past 20 years I have examined the research on the impact of film and television on reading and writing. Almost all the studies have fallen into the following two contradictory categories: Some empiricists claim great harm is done by the media; others claim that assertions of harm are extremely overblown. In her study of television, Neuman (1991) best summarized the new friendly empirical attitude about the media in the following way:

> Indeed, rather than banish new technologies, we must rejoice in the marvel of expanding knowledge bases, and explore ways of using this larger network of information to enrich children's lives and further their understanding of what it means to be truly literate. (p. 202)

Despite Neuman's optimism, other empirical researchers do not share this view. Recent newspaper reports of new studies indicate children are at great risk because of the heavy doses of violence found in television and film (Carter, 1996). There are theorists who believe the damaging impact of the media is greatest on children from the lowest socioeconomic groups (Greenfield, 1984).

No side clearly wins in the empirical conclusions on the impact of media. The only fair summary one can make from an overview of the research was made by Stephen Kline (1993), who indicated how difficult it is to empirically trace the impact of media violence on children. After all, Kline noted, the effects of television on children remain difficult to trace because such effects depend on how children interpret fiction—that is, how they make sense of the context of the violent act within the narrative framework that explains and justifies it. Rather than attempting to quantify the impact of media, perhaps it is more beneficial to speculate about that impact and study the emotional and experiential aspects from a philosophical point of view, as Kubey and Csikszentmihalyi (1990) recommend.

I have found no definitive trend that emerges from the empirical research on the impact of media. Perhaps the only claim that can be inferred from the research is that the media is powerful. This is my basic premise for analyzing and teaching the electronic media.

Schools in the Shadow of Film and Television

People in today's society incorporate media into every aspect of their lives. Educated people require media to complete their emotional and intellectual knowledge of the world. These people also need full access to all media and an understanding of the good and bad inherent in the media's messages. The world has changed, even if some schools will not admit it. I no longer can envision survival without understanding film and television.

However, I also cannot envision fulfilling lives without written books, magazines, or journals, because all students need written texts, too. If they only are relating to image-producing texts and their world is mediated only through film and television, students will be crippled. They will be underemployed in a workforce demanding high-level print literacy skills; they will be socially at risk, saturated by undifferentiated, seductive images they neither will understand nor be able to control. Our students need to understand and produce written texts to contribute fully to society, intellectually, economically, socially, and morally. Also, they must use written texts to understand the media, to provide an intellectual framework and schema by which to manage the ubiquitous electronic media.

Ignoring the media as a part of the curriculum is an extreme form of denial. It is like denying the existence of the most powerful communication mode since writing. However, many educators do deny it, dismissing the media as a mindless wasteland. Our students know better and would be better served if we shed light on this form of communication. These are my goals:

1. To transform students into discriminating television and film viewers who can distinguish good from bad, exploitation from communication.

2. To sensitize students so they perceive how television and film are designed to influence and manipulate them.

3. To educate students to understand television and film visually and thematically, so they can analyze and critique the media they watch.

4. To develop critical awareness so students can distinguish the very worst of the electronic media and can devote their time to other pursuits.

5. To develop in students an aesthetic appreciation for the finest the electronic media has to offer.

Using Speaking, Reading, and Writing to Teach Film and Television

Fuller (1996) has addressed why media studies never caught on in the United States. English teachers, more so than ever, are afraid to be accused of teaching frivolous subject matter. The educational atmosphere is stifled; too many government programs make it difficult for teachers to change the curriculum away from anything other than traditional English curricula like *Julius Caesar* and grammar worksheets. Even though many studies call for media to be studied in schools, the irony is that few teachers can risk it without incurring local criticism. Neither the government, nor researchers, nor educators have made U.S. classrooms hospitable places for the study of media.

When I taught high school I taught a course on the media. Now that I teach college I know a few sympathetic high school teachers willing to teach media, but not many. However, I continue to teach teenagers about the media in a summer institute in which I use speaking, reading, and writing activities. I have done this for several years, so I have a curriculum that has been tested on real students. I will describe here some of the activities I have done with the hope that teachers can adapt them to the classes of most U.S. high schools. I also hope that teachers who realize the need to teach media will be able to incorporate these activities into the regular English curriculum. I hope someday American schools will become forward thinking enough to expand the curriculum to include the serious study of media. I remain optimistic.

What often strikes me when I talk to my adolescent students is how so many of them know every movie and express their knowledge of them enthusiastically. They also know television, but they are more selective about it, with only some shows "cool" enough to watch. Movies are a big social event for adolescents, particularly young teenagers who are driven to movie theaters by friends or parents.

All movies are influential, particularly with young viewers, so I make it a point to see a popular new release in a theater with my summer students. We go together, watch the movie, and then go back to my house for a hot dog roast. Although we never formally study the film we have just seen, we have informal discussions throughout the evening. Often, the films we see this way are entertaining and riveting, but many provide an evening's worth of entertainment with some mediated images, but are soon forgotten. However, the movies I use in my classroom are selected because they are powerful resources to study one or more aspects of media. The films I select hold up over time.

FIGURE 1: Letter to Parents

Dear Parent or Guardian:

This course is designed to study television and film literacy. With the aid of a series of films and videotapes, we will probe how the electronic media informs, entertains, and manipulates. Students will participate in several activities that will help accomplish the major goal of this unit: to create visually literate and perceptive viewers who are capable of withstanding the constant barrage of media propaganda, viewers who are capable of understanding how the media shapes our world, and who can appreciate the media as a major artistic achievement of this century.

Included among the films I plan to use are *Glory* and *The Player*. Both films are rated R and contain language and situations that may be offensive to some viewers. However, I feel it is important to analyze and understand how these powerful films impact teenagers, one of the largest film audiences in America. If you feel your daughter, son, or dependent should not see these films, please inform me as soon as possible so I can make alternative arrangements.

Sincerely,

Hal Foster

A Rationale for Using R-Rated Films in Classrooms—But Be Careful

Many of my classroom movies are rated R due to sexual or violent content. I send letters to the students' parents explaining what films I am using and why I am using these films. An example of the letter is shown in Figure 1.

My hopes are that parents will understand clearly the benefits of having their children see these films with guidance, and in most cases parents agree with me. On one occasion a student's parents asked me not to show the films to their daughter and I agreed. This situation worked out fine, yet I know that using films in the classroom must be done carefully. Teachers who use films in the classroom are vulnerable and are subject to attack. For instance, a teacher in Antelope, California was fired for showing *Dead Poet's Society* (Wallis, 1996). Also, the classroom use of Zeffirelli's *Romeo and Juliet* sometimes provokes protest because of a scene in which some viewers imagine a bit of flesh. *Schindler's List*, perhaps one of the most thoughtful and profoundly human films ever made, received more protests in 1994 than any other film used in classrooms (Wallis, 1996).

It is no wonder why teachers are skeptical about teaching media. I advise all teachers to be careful, make sure to get permission from a principal or department chair, and be prepared to defend the film they use on thematic and moral grounds.

I believe strongly in using certain films in my classroom (see Figure 2 for a list of some of the films used in my summer class). It is no secret that a child of any age either can rent R-rated films or see them in a theater. So, it is better to see some of the more powerful films with adult supervision. The films I choose deal with large issues and mediate strong experiences. These films compete with reading, yet enhance reading by adding to the emotional base of readers. These films also serve as catalysts for reading by motivating reading about the films and about the subjects of these films. The films also can stimulate writing, about the subjects covered by the film and about the film itself. Strong film experiences are very much like strong book experiences, in that both stimulate the desire for more viewing, reading, and analysis. My class does more activities after these films, which can inspire some very lively debate and discussion.

FIGURE 2: My Film List

The Breakfast Club	*The Graduate*
Broadcast News	*A League of Their Own*
Citizen Kane	*Much Ado About Nothing*
Do the Right Thing	*The Player*
Field of Dreams	*Schindler's List*
Glory	*To Kill a Mockingbird*

Speaking, Reading, and Writing Activities for the Media Classroom

Background

I expect my students to have a basic background in the art of film and television. Thus, I teach the following concepts before we ever discuss these forms of media:

- *Composition*: The objects, people, and places that are seen within the camera shot.
- *Movement*: Motion in films takes many forms. It may mean the movement of people or objects within the shot or the movement of the camera, such as a pan or a tracking shot.
- *Editing*: The process of cutting and splicing film. This is one of the most technical and aesthetic processes of creating motion picture art.
- *Sound*: Music, dialogue, and background noise.
- *Lighting and color*: Carefully used to create feelings and moods, similar to a painting (adapted from Foster, 1979).

Leading a Film Discussion

I have used the film *Glory* for response-based discussions. In normal 40- to 50-minute class periods *Glory* will take about three or four periods—not the ideal way to see a movie, but satisfactory if there is not time for showing it in one sitting.

Before the movie. I tell a bit about the Civil War and the history of the black brigade depicted in the movie before the class views it. I then give instructions to watch and enjoy the film, and I say nothing else. I believe strongly that people should reflect on film experiences only after they have seen the movie. Films are meant to be watched uncritically, so I never instruct students to watch for anything specific in the film.

After the movie. I do not discuss the film immediately after the movie; first comes the journal writing. I write the following questions on the board for the writing activity:

- Did you feel the white officers treated the black officers with respect? Yes? No? Maybe? Why?
- Why were the black soldiers so motivated to fight?
- Could you tell from this movie why Civil War battles cost so many lives?
- How would you describe the living conditions of the men during the training?
- Can you describe the music and how it created moods during the film?
- Do you remember how lighting and color were used to create viewer feelings in the last battle scene?
- How did movement (camera and crowd) increase the excitement during the battle scenes?
- Do you like the movie? Why or why not? (adapted from Foster, 1994)

In some cases, instead of journal writing I may ask students to work with the film and television analysis sheet shown in Figure 3.

I am a firm believer that good classroom discussions need the structure that is listed in Figure 3. Now that my students have thought about the film, have seen it, and have written about it, they are ready to discuss it.

All I have to do is to ask, "What do you think?" If that does not work I can ask any of the specific questions from the journal writing or from the analysis sheet. If my students are comfortable with one another and with me they will discuss the film now. This system has been successful most of the time.

Media Panels

One of the early foci of the ninth-grade media class is panel discussions.

Panel Topics

- Good movies; bad movies; film reviews that consider entertainment, values, quality, and art.

- Good television; bad television; how television works. Is it good for us or bad for us? Why?

- Children's television: What is good for children and what is bad for children? Why?

- Television commercials: How do they work? Are they good for us or bad for us? Why?

- How television has changed music; how music uses television.

- Make your own topic (with teacher approval).

FIGURE 3: Film and Television Analysis Sheet

Structural questions
- How does the editing affect the mood of the viewer?
- Does the lighting elicit a mood? How?
- Does the movement excite or calm the viewer? Neither? How?
- How do the images help create the mood?
- How are colors used to create atmosphere or mood?
- Do the music and background noises add to the general atmosphere?

Social questions
- How do the people dress?
- How would you characterize the behavior of the people?
- What ages are the people?
- How would you characterize the general appearance of the people?
- How do the characters relate to one another?
- What are the economic circumstances of the characters?
- What methods do the characters use to solve their problems?
- Describe the family situations that are shown.

Mythological considerations
- What does the movie, program, or commercial imply about the following? Consider any of the following:

love sex nature success failure pride death marriage
friendship family teamwork the individual work play men
women children fun adventure possessions appearance
leisure reading knowledge home life

Adapted from *Crossing Over: Whole Language for Secondary English Teachers*, by H. Foster, 1994, p. 211.

The Rules

- The panels are a talk show format.
- The student host gives a short monologue about the topic, about five minutes.
- The expert guests give short responses defining their positions on the topic, about five minutes each.
- The host elicits responses and statements from the student audience.
- Everyone in class will serve as a host, a guest, and a member of the audience.
- Each participant will prepare a one-page written statement about a topic. These will serve as a basis for the opening statement.
- Each participant will prepare three to five questions for the audience to serve as a basis for discussion.
- Each participant must use at least one library reference and refer to at least one of the in-class films.
- Panelists may interview the teacher for part of the response.

The Resources

I use two films to introduce the panels. The films are *Broadcast News* and *The Player*; both have adult themes and are rated R. I give students a focus question and journal questions for each film. After showing the films I allow my students to freewrite about the movies using the questions, then we discuss the films. The point is to use the films for reference in the panel discussions when the topics are appropriate. In this way, my students learn about the media by seeing two films on the media. They experience these films, interact with them, and use them for reference. The following activity is my example of how classrooms can tap into the vast resources offered by film and television. This activity broadens references beyond print and reflects the true nature of modern learning.

Broadcast News. Focus question for students: What does this movie tell us about how television news is made?

I expected this film to be the easier of the two because of its straightforward nature. The movie depicts a network news team and deals with serious ethical issues about how news is written and presented. The film gives a strong behind-the-scenes view of the news and demonstrates that ratings are more important than news worthiness. Also, a mature love triangle weaves throughout this movie.

Reaction to Broadcast News. My students found *Broadcast News* to be helpful on many levels. First, it gave them tips on how to look and talk when they put on their newscast (the culminating exercise of the class). My students gained real insights into what to wear and how to wear it in front of a camera. They learned how to speak their lines, which words to "punch," and how to make eye contact with the camera. They learned that television news is not only about news but also about who delivers the news and what the newscaster looks like. They learned about the art of news writing and news delivery. Through this film they gained dramatic and emotional insight into the infrastructure of news delivery.

What aspects of the movie did not work with the class? "Too much yuppie whining," my students complained. The love story taxed them. Many students found the love triangle to be tiresome. They were excellent critics. The love story was long and it was the part that was hardest for me to watch repeatedly. The parts about the news had great pacing; they were filled with energy and strong camera work.

The Player. Focus question for students: Are filmmakers really this rotten? If yes, are the movies they make rotten as well?

I expected *The Player* to be a harder film for teenagers to watch, because it is darker and more complex. The plot is not straightforward and the film is long and somewhat experimental, particularly with the use of sound. The movie presents a very cynical and dark view of filmmaking. The film may be classified more as satirical than realistic, but it does present a provocative view of American filmmaking, one that exposes the ruthless competition to find good stories that will appeal to the largest audience. Filmmaking in *The Player* is not an art; it is a crass business aimed at the lowest tastes of the American public and one that views the public in the dumbest possible light.

Reaction to **The Player.** The ninth graders who saw this film loved it. They were not bothered in the least by the cynicism or the complexity. They easily accepted the view of American filmmaking as cynical and accepted the opinion that Hollywood is filled with conceited, evil people who exploit the American public. The sexual content is very heavy for ninth graders, but they handled it with my help. We discussed these scenes as part of the movie, and the class understood how seductiveness was an important attribute of the lead character. I felt that the movie was a learning experience for my students, teaching them about how movies are made to make money with no concern for the subject matter. They also learned about the mechanics of production: how movies are pitched, how scripts are evaluated, how much competition exists in the film industry, the role of the producer, the problems writers encounter, where stories come from, and how executives are hired.

Film Journal Questions

Students were asked to use the following questions on page 185 as a basis for incorporating the two films into their panel discussions.

- Does/can television provide an accurate picture of the world?
- What motivates people who work in the media?
- Are television and movie stories bad/good/neither for us?
- Do movies and television shape our lives? How/why?
- Do these movies work with teenagers?
- How do you rate these movies? Good/bad; 5-point scale. Explain.

Results of the Panels

The panels worked well. They brought out provocative issues and began our dialogue on the media. This opened our course on film and television and set the framework for what we would study in depth. The films we saw provided us with a base to understand film and television and were our first look at the language of film and television and how it works. We were starting on the road to become literates of the 1990s and beyond.

More Classroom Activities

Analyzing Television News

My students watch two different network newscasts, both videotaped on the same night. Then they are asked to complete the sheet shown in Figure 4 as the basis for discussion.

Making a Newscast

The culminating experience of the media course is to have my students make a newscast. These are the steps:

1. Select roles based on real newscasts, such as anchor, weatherperson, sports reporter, news reporter, or commentator.

FIGURE 4: News Program Criteria Sheet

	Program 1	Program 2
Length of opening story		
Nature of opening story		
Number of commercials		
Time on anchor		
Time on news film		
Number of stories		

News Analysis

Describe the set

Describe the clothing of the
anchor or anchors

Describe the voice of the anchor

What is the main story?

How is the main story depicted?

What is the most interesting
story other than the main
story? Why?

What is the softest story
of the newscast?

How is this story covered?

Write a few words that
describe the newscast.

Describe the newscast in terms
of the following:

Editing

Composition

(continued)

FIGURE 4: News Program Criteria Sheet (continued)

Lighting

Color

Sound

Movement

What kinds of commercials
are shown on the newscast?

Who is the audience for these
commercials?

Adapted from *Crossing Over: Whole Language for Secondary English Teachers*,
by H. Foster, 1994, p. 215.

2. Divide class into newscast teams.

3. Have each team write either a spoof or a real newscast based on newspapers and magazines.

4. Rehearse the newscast at least two times. Do screen testing. Make tapes of individuals delivering the news and evaluate them based on how professionals perform. (I do not let groups watch one another rehearse.)

5. Tape each newscast. Either bring a camera into the classroom or take the class to a real television studio (if possible). Many college campuses have professional facilities. The more professionally taped the newscast is, the better the experience is for the students. (I do not let teams watch one another being taped.)

6. Show the tapes. Compare how students do with real newscasts. Discuss the difficulties and challenges of actually appearing on television.

Reading and Writing in the Shadow of Film and Television

By using language to understand the media, people become better at reading, writing, and speaking. It is a cycle; the more you learn about media, the more literate you become. Writing and reading are a major part of media literacy. If we can show students how their lives are mediated through film and television, maybe we can convince them to broaden their relationship with all media, including reading and writing. Then they will become part of the truly literate world: a world that reads and writes, watches television, sees film, and explores the World Wide Web, doing all of these activities for entertainment and information. But students also will understand that the media are mediated experiences that provide only part of the truth and part of the answers. No medium gives the whole truth, but all forms of media are useful tools in helping to create complete and fulfilling lives. As literacy and the world change, the challenge is to add to our sources of entertainment and knowledge, not to abandon the media that provides us the best access to reason and critical thinking—reading and writing.

References

Atwell, N. (1987). *In the middle: Writing, reading, and learning with adolescents*. Portsmouth, NH: Heinemann.

Carter, B. (1996, February 7). New report becomes a weapon in the debate over TV violence. *The New York Times*, p. A1, B5.

Foster, H. (1979). *The new literacy: The language of film and television*. Urbana, IL: National Council of Teachers of English.

Foster, H. (1994). *Crossing over: Whole language for secondary English teachers*. Fort Worth, TX: Harcourt Brace.

Fuller, L. (1996). Media education: Where have we been? Where are we going? *English Education, 28*, 58–66.

Greenfield, P. (1984). *Mind and media: The effects of television, video games, and computers*. Cambridge, MA: Harvard University Press.

Kline, S. (1993). *Out of the garden*. New York: Verso.

Kubey, R., & Csikszentmihalyi, M. (1990). *Television and the quality of life: How viewing shapes everyday experience*. Hillsdale, NJ: Erlbaum.

Neuman, S. (1991). *Literacy in the television age*. Norwood, NJ: Ablex.

Purves, A. (1994). People prose. In R. Fox (Ed.), *Images in language, media and mind* (pp. 21–28). Urbana, IL: National Council of Teachers of English.

Real, M. (1989). *Super media: A cultural studies approach*. Newbury Park, CA: Sage.

Rose, M. (1989). *Lives on the boundary: The struggles and achievements of America's underprepared*. New York: Free Press.

Wallis, D. (1996, February 18). I will not show R-rated films in school, I will not.... *The New York Times*, p. H25.

CHAPTER 10

The Future of the Written Word

LAWRENCE BAINES

> The fact that the image of the world is receding from the communicative grasp of the word has had its impact on the quality of language. As western consciousness has become less dependent on the resources of language to order experience and conduct the business of the mind, the words themselves seem to have lost some of their precision and vitality. (Steiner, 1984, p. 295)

The written word is receding as our communications device of choice. That is the verdict of luminaries such as Birkerts (1990, 1994), Kernan (1990), Ong (1967, 1982), Postman (1992, 1995), Steiner (1984), Stoll (1995), and others who have noted that much of the technological innovation that has occurred since 1950 represents a move toward image-based and electronically mediated messages and a move away from words and books. Implicit in the criticism over the explosion of technology is the idea that without linguistically rich media, there will be little chance that children will master the language. The fear of many teachers and writers is that as the corpus of language shrinks, so shrinks the human capacity for complex thought.

Film, video, television, and the Internet have altered the ways students learn and have affected their attitudes toward learning. Teachers of reading and English today are in the delicate position of having to learn an entirely different set of pedagogical approaches, although they still are expected to promote the kinds of literacies that always have been considered their domain—writing, reading, speaking, listening, and thinking. Although these literacies demand linguistic competence, the electronic media, which captures the attention of most students, is image based; words (such as dialogue in a film, or text in a World Wide Web site) often only supplement visual messages.

In this chapter, I will review six trends that are manifestations of the retreat of the written word:

1. The power of image-based media to influence thought and behavior;
2. The tendency of newer technologies to obliterate aspects of older technologies;
3. The current emphasis on school reform;
4. The influences of advertising and marketing;
5. The current state of books as repositories of the language; and
6. The reconceptualization of the library.

The Retreat of the Written Word

The Power of Image-Based Media to Influence Thought and Behavior

When individuals feel that their relationships are dissatisfying for external or unstable reasons, then they might expect and receive certain gratifications from the media. (Canary & Spitzberg, 1993, p. 817)

It is interesting to consider that while the communications industry pours millions of dollars into research pertaining to gratifications and uses of media, many educators choose to ignore the influence of nonprint media on the formulation of a student's values, goals, and aspirations. Most contemporary media research has embraced the idea of the viewer as an active communicator (Anderson & Anderson, 1993; Rubin, 1993; Scholle, 1991) and assumes that human beings look to media for the satisfaction of some of their real or perceived needs.

After racially motivated riots in the United States, the criminal and civil trials of O.J. Simpson, and the public eruptions over films that address race and religion in a controversial manner, such as *Colors* (1988), *Boyz N the Hood* (1992), *Do the Right Thing* (1989), and *The Last Temptation of Christ* (1988), the position that film and television do not influence behavior seems indefensible. Viewing film, video, and television has been shown to affect students' cognitive, affective, and behavioral processes—their attitudes toward violence (Bandura, 1968; Linz, 1989; Oliver, 1993); the development of childhood phobias (Cantor, 1991; Cantor & Reilly, 1982, Sarafino, 1986); sensual arousal (Hansen & Krygowsi, 1994); their attitudes toward political candidates (Eisenman, Girdner, Burroughs, & Routman, 1993); and their attitudes toward the elderly (Cross, 1989).

Not surprisingly, the relationship between what is viewed in the media and what is perceived as reality is quite strong. For example, most of the public's knowledge about AIDS has been gleaned from advertisements and television programs (Herog & Far, 1995). People who view television soap operas on a regular basis believe that there is a greater incidence of crime and marital discord in society and believe that there are more doctors and lawyers in the workforce than nonviewers of soap operas (Shrum, 1995). Through their omnipresence, image-based media have the unique power to influence and reflect public opinion.

In a study of the evolution of family comedies on U.S. network television, Douglas and Olson (1996) found a disturbing trend in the quality of family life depicted on programs that air during "prime time" viewing hours. Contemporary television series depicted more conflict between children and parents, less sensitivity among family members, and a marked increase in selfish behavior. When considering the effects of media on student behavior, it is useful to remember the following comment from Csikszentmihalyi (1996): "One song heard on the radio...can have a more profound effect on a child's future than a thousand hours spent in school" (p. 108).

The Tendency of Newer Technologies to Obliterate Aspects of Older Technologies

> The biggest news in books in 1994 was not a single event but rather a trend: the growth of electronic publishing. (Chism, 1994, p. 37A)

The time Americans spend reading has declined over the years. In 1993, the average adult spent 1,080 hours watching network television stations, 449 hours watching cable television, 248 hours listening to recorded music, 61 hours watching prerecorded video or commercial films in theaters, 170 hours reading daily newspapers, 85 hours reading magazines, and 99 hours reading books (U.S. Department of Commerce, 1995). Translating this data into the actual time spent with print and nonprint media, for every hour an adult spends reading, 5.2 hours are spent viewing and listening. Results from studies of adolescents by Csikszentmihalyi

(1984, 1993a, 1993b) indicate that the habits of teens are very similar to those of adults.

One of the more interesting ways that a newer technology can obliterate an older one is the case of a book being made into a film. The release of a relatively unpopular, critically denounced film such as *The Scarlet Letter* (1995) can boost sales of a classic book dramatically. As films that are based on books are released, the covers of paperbacks are changed accordingly so that they reflect the advertising campaign for the film. For example, Hawthorne's somber romance *The Scarlet Letter* (1850) becomes a love story with a photo of the two main characters embracing on the cover. Recent paperback versions of Austen's *Sense and Sensibility* (1811), adapted into a film in 1995, portray a simple, good-hearted love story. Boorstin (1962) described the phenomenon of films overpowering books when he noted the disintegration of the author in the Broadway presentation of *Ben Hur* in 1959:

> The detailed printed program listed everybody from Sam Zimbalist, the producer, to Joan Bridge who was Color Consultant for Costumes, and Gabriella Borzelli, the hair stylist. But it nowhere listed the name of Lew Wallace, the author. (p. 152)

Today, movies are just one possibility among a throng of media competing for time in students' lives. The fundamental shift away from printed text becomes obvious when the continued decline in circulation of almost every major American newspaper is contrasted against the surge in computer ownership and Internet usage (Quality Education Data, 1995; Williams, 1996). Paging through the infinite collection of images and sounds on the Internet, one develops a sense of being thoroughly modern and competent.

An interesting CD-ROM (Limbreglia & Bernhardt, 1995) depicting the life and works of Jack Kerouac illustrates

how images can overwhelm words. On the CD-ROM are lo-
cated the following:

- *The Gallery*—paintings by Kerouac and paintings of
  him and his circle.
- *The Archive*—a collection of letters, diaries, and
  artifacts.
- *Jack Kerouac Sampler*—recordings of selections from
  Kerouac's writings read by Kerouac and others.
- *Life and Times*—a year by year graphic chronology
  of Kerouac's life and writings.
- *Jack Kerouac and the San Francisco Beats*—an interactive graphical chart of relationships among major
  literary figures of the Beat generation.
- *The Dharma Bums*—the entire text of the novel
  "fully searchable and heavily annotated with text,
  audio, visual, and video links."
- *Extras*—easy access to all the audio and video clips
  of the CD-ROM.

Which are the segments of the CD-ROM that you would first
investigate? Most English teachers would likely choose to
browse the paintings, photos, audio clips, film footage, and
graphs before deciding to go to the text of *The Dharma Bums*.
Only two of the seven sections on the CD-ROM actually involve what Kerouac wrote. Even the text of *The Dharma Bums*
is dense with "clickable links" so that a reader may add ani-
mation, music, and sound to bolster the otherwise unelabo-
rated text. In CD-ROMs like this, words serve as prompts for
the more exciting prospect of a multimedia experience.

The Current Emphasis on School Reform

Two movements in educational reform are weakening
the grasp of the written word: (1) the idea of multiple intelli-

(MI), and (2) the effort to make schools into centers for technology. Of course, neither of these theories are horrible prospects; on the contrary, they hold great promise for helping to individualize instruction and to more fully integrate the knowledge from other disciplines into the language arts and reading curricula. Nevertheless, in the limited school day, the more time spent on drawing or playing with hypertext means that less time is available for reading and writing.

The idea of multiple intelligences. Concerning the drive toward incorporating the idea of multiple intelligences in the classroom, Gardner (1993) wrote the following:

> There are now several educators in the land who give regular workshops on "MI theory," as well as a number of organizations that highlight an "MI perspective." There are dozens of graphic renditions of the MI array, dozens of popular articles about the theory, a growing shelf of books, and even a regular magazine. (p. xiii)

I remember wincing when I first read Gardner's *Frames of Mind: The Theory of Multiple Intelligences* (1983). I had just finished a year in which I taught three sections of English and three sections of world history at a middle school in Texas, and I was convinced that, in general, most students read poorly, wrote poorly, and were apathetic about the prospect of expending effort to improve these skills. I thought that Gardner's hypothesis that individuals actually possess seven different kinds of intelligences, not just the two given the most attention in schools and on assessments—linguistic and mathematical— was a mixed blessing. Certainly, the idea of multiple intelligences would open the possibilities of having teachers acknowledge the diverse talents of their students. But, what worried me was the possibility of teachers and students finding justification for retreating even further from books and words. Getting students to consent to read selections from my contemporary collection of young adult books had been daunting enough. I was afraid that Gardner's work would undermine what little success I had experienced in getting students to read and would give them (and their parents) some substantiation for abandoning books for more entertaining media.

The next year I had a parent-teacher conference that helped give credence to my fear. The conference involved a student, James, who had failed to turn in more than half the assignments for the most recent grading period. I began by telling James's mother, Ms. Kane, what I believed to be at the core of his problem—his laziness. I said, "James sits in class, looks out the window, and draws pictures in his notebook when he should be reading, writing, or listening."

Ms. Kane was a caring, well-educated, assertive woman with a booming voice. "You folks just do not know how to teach James," she informed me. "In case you don't know, James is at the genius level in practically everything. He just gets bored with your emphasis on repetitive, rote, linguistic tasks."

"There's little rote or repetitive about my class," I replied, in an attempt to defend myself. "I have students self-select many of their books and give them as much room to maneuver as I can for their writing assignments. Although James may be smart and capable, he just sits in class and does nothing."

"James is an innovative thinker, " Ms. Kane retorted. "I don't think just because you value *mere words* over real experience, art, and other intelligences is any reason to punish James. Howard Gardner says...."

Mere words. The phrase is haunting in its implications. Although one might argue over the details of Gardner's theory of multiple intelligences, it is undeniable that an aptitude with words still is valued in the academic community. Concomitant with the rush toward portfolio and alternative assessments, secondary students increasingly must take a state-mandated high school competency exam that includes an assessment of linguistic competence. To gain entrance into undergraduate and graduate programs of study, most postsecondary institutions in the United States still require the Scholastic Assessment Test (SAT), American College Test (ACT), Graduate Record Examination (GRE), Graduate Management Admissions Test (GMAT), and other tests that claim to assess word knowledge (Singal, 1991).

Schools as centers of technology. Another factor that has contributed to the depletion of the written word is the mania for bringing the cutting edge of technology into schools. For the past 20 years, school budgets have been cut, capital improvements have been postponed, and teacher salaries have remained stagnant, yet expenditures for technology in schools have soared (Quality Education Data, 1996). The increases in technology spending have been fueled by some unverified findings that support technology uses in the classroom. The following statements are examples:

> Students participating in classrooms using videodisc instruction achieve more than students who are taught using traditional science instructional practices. (Rock & Cummings, 1994, p. 49)

> Technology supports the active learning that produces academic results and the habits of mind essential for current and future requirements of the family, citizenship, and employability. (Boysen, 1996, p. 56)

> One of the best documented successes with computers in education is in developing students' writing. (Peck & Dorricott, 1994, p. 12)

After reading some of the claims regarding achievement gains attributable to technology, one can hardly be surprised that some schools have adopted improvement plans that focus on technological solutions. These plans often are implemented as if all a teacher has to do is roll several computers into each classroom, sit back, and wait for miraculous gains in achievement. Yet, there is no legitimate basis for claiming that instruction delivered over a computer is superior to other kinds of instruction, such as one-on-one interaction between teacher and student (Baines, 1997a, 1997c; Clark 1983, 1985, 1991, 1994).

Most secondary teachers claim that they use computers and other electronic media extensively in their classrooms (Quality Education Data, 1996). At the postsecondary level, nearly one in four classes is held in computer-equipped classrooms (Deloughry, 1996). A recent series of grants from the U.S. Department of Education has offered millions to school districts that desire help with the integration of computer technology.

Often, advertisers of new textbooks emphasize the technological advantages of their products, especially multimedia supplements and computer-based lessons. In fact, a recent trend is for many school districts to purchase computer software, CD-ROMs, and videodiscs in lieu of textbooks. In the descriptions of the two textbook series that follow, note that the publisher uses multimedia experiences to bolster the appeal of words or to replace them altogether.

> The "Read to Me" choice lets the children listen to the book with spoken dialogue and animation. The "Let Me Play" choice allows children to browse through the book in any order, and to click buttons on any page to bring animation to characters and objects. (Wepner, Seminoff, & Blanchard, 1996, p. 28)

> Designed with K–2 students in mind, it [the Muppet Slate word-processing program] allows incorporation of simple graphics into text. For example, a child can insert a picture

of an elephant into a line of text instead of writing the word "elephant." (Thornburg, 1989, p. 91)

Although books are supposed to be repositories of the written word, at times one wonders if it is not "print media that are leading the way in pushing books off the map" (Franzen, 1996, p. 38). Undeniably, today a writer is much more likely to find work writing for CD-ROM than writing for literary or commercial journals (Roberts, 1996).

The Influences of Advertising and Marketing

> We have entered the world of Disney, and I am seized by the fear that there might be no way out. (Birkerts, 1994, p. 29)

Like it or not, films for children have the power to influence what a child wears, what a child eats, what a child writes on (and with), what a child reads, and what a child does in his or her time outside of school. Indeed, one popular activity today is for children to view a favorite videotape repeatedly—sometimes hundreds of times.

Students live in a world inundated by corporate-controlled, electronically mediated messages. Cutlip (1995) found that 40% of modern "newscasts" consist of items created by corporate-sponsored press agencies and public relations bureaus. These public relations messages are rarely, if ever, altered by journalists. Public relations firms and advertising companies have had a profound impact on the style and content of television, film, and politics. Music Television (MTV) is as complete a hybrid of the quick cuts, explosive hits, and subjective viewpoint of advertising as one could hope to find. The degree to which public relations firms have been employed to mold American opinion about global warming, tobacco, health care, and chemical alteration of food products through the media is related by Stauber and Rampton (1996).

Politics, especially, has been changed permanently by the electronic media and advertising. Today, a candidate who cannot look confident, attractive, and competent in front of the camera has absolutely no chance to win an election. Indeed, the contrast between the U.S. senatorial debates of 1858 when Abraham Lincoln and Stephen Douglas exchanged oral barbs outdoors during a hot Illinois summer is in stark contrast to today's politics in which well-rehearsed candidates with staffs of advisors and speechwriters do battle in preformatted debates and in 20-second television advertisements. Political platforms are condensed into easily understandable sound bytes, filled with visuals and emotional appeal, such as "The time is now," "A vote for America," "For the people," "A president we can trust," and "For a change." Again, the complexity of language is reduced and the cultivation of image takes precedence.

Books as Repositories of the Written Word

Shortly before his death in 1983, Tennessee Williams spoke about the compromises in language a screenwriter is forced to make to accommodate the realities of making a film:

> First they put me on *Marriage Is a Private Affair* for Lana Turner. Well, they expressed great delight with my dialogue, and I think it was good. But they said, "You give Miss Turner too many multisyllable words!" So I said, "Well, some words do contain more than one syllable!" And Pandro Berman, who loved me very much—Lana Turner just happened to be his girlfriend at the time—he said to me, "Tennessee, Lana can tackle two syllables, but I'm afraid if you go into three you're taxing her vocabulary!" (1989, p. 255)

In an examination of the language of novels and their adaptations, I (1996, 1997b) concluded that films tend to use fewer polysyllabic words, have less complex sentence structures, have less lexical diversity, and reduce the complexity of dialogue, plot, character, and theme. The view until now has been that books hold the cumulative knowledge of the world and that it is writers—not movie producers—who offer the most worthwhile meditative experiences. Dinsmore (1937) emphasizes the importance of writers in the following excerpt:

> The poets who dealt most extensively with human struggles in the extreme moments stress most insistently and powerfully that there is a quality in the human spirit that is superior to disaster, that "feeds on death," that is sublimely above all the reaches of the malignity of evil, that distills wisdom from sorrow, finds wells of refreshment in the darkest valleys, extracts beauty from ashes and oil from the flinty rocks of difficulty.... Common is the belief in help from the Unseen, and the sense that the meaning of life has not been fully disclosed during the years of our mortality. (p. 247)

It is difficult to imagine that a media critic today would write that television, film, and the Internet were "above all the reaches of the malignity of evil." The nonprint media constantly presents vivid footage of the world's most disturbing atrocities; these images appear in front of us with a press of a button.

Book publishing, long the trusted repository of the word, is changing to accommodate the proliferation of the image. As a matter of survival, most publishers have incorporated electronic publishing (such as CD-ROM, audio books, and multimedia packages). Even the bestseller lists are inundated with the influence of nonprint media. For example, although the best-selling books of 1982 and 1983 were picture books derived from the films *E.T. The Extra-Terrestrial* and *Return of the Jedi*, the three best-selling hardcover non-fiction books of 1993 were written by media personalities Rush Limbaugh, Jerry Seinfeld, and Howard Stern (*Publishers Weekly*, March 7, 1994). Eight of the ten best-selling children's books of 1990 depicted the adventures of the Teenage Mutant Ninja Turtles (Englehardt, 1991). However, R.L. Stine has supplanted this children's literature with a series of shocking stories for children of all ages. Stine currently is the United States' best-selling author (adult, young adult, or otherwise), with more than 90 million books in print (West, 1995). The following is a brief segment from Stine's (1995) *The Cataluna Chronicles: Deadly Fire*:

> William raised the ax.
>
> So heavy. So heavy. Too heavy.
>
> It fell from his hand.
>
> The pain roared through his body. The teeth cut into his throat. He could feel the steady throb of the blood as it poured out.
>
> Poured out. Flowed out.

If books receive any attention by the public or the media today, they usually are books that serve as only one product line in a multifaceted marketing campaign. Writer T. Coraghessan Boyle admits that reading and books have been kept alive largely through the efforts of teachers in secondary and postsecondary institutions. Boyle (1996) wrote, "The academy has sort of preserved us as a viable subject. I mean, people aren't really buying Chaucer today either, but he's preserved, thank God, for our culture. Writing in this generation has moved into the academic arena" (p. 50).

When writers begin writing things such as, "I don't read books anymore.... Film is my faithful love" (Fernandez, 1993, p. 8); "Words are...awkward instruments, and they will be laid aside eventually, probably sooner than we think" (Burroughs, 1989, p. 352); and "I still maintain there comes a point when one 'outgrows' novels, at least in the sense that the words no longer speak to one's experience in a way that reveals new depth about that experience" (Krystal, 1996, p. 58), it is easy to conclude that books are in trouble.

The Reconceptualization of the Library

Most urban and university libraries have replaced card catalogues with online computers (Baker, 1996). Not surprisingly, such a transformation has meant that about 40% of library budgets now go toward the purchase of technology—mainly for the purchase and maintenance of Internet-capable computers and terminals that provide information concerning the library's holdings, as well as access to a variety of databases. Indeed, most librarians caught in the dilemma of choosing between "going electronic" or maintaining the number of new print-and-paper acquisitions have felt compelled to choose computers. Networked computers are not just perceived as nice extras, but are assumed to provide a whole new infrastructure for libraries.

Most contemporary librarians perceive the library as an information center that exists to serve the community, not just a building that houses stacks of books and magazines. Indeed, public libraries routinely hold community events, such as "children's storytime," musical events, and town meetings. Although such willingness to serve the community is commendable, Tisdale (1997) argues that libraries have gone beyond the idea of the community information center to the construct of "library as entertainment center." Tisdale wrote,

> Once you buy the premise that information—and entertaining information—is the point, you have to buy the equipment, even if it is a Faustian deal.... The [new li-

brary]...will have hundreds of Internet stations...but it won't have a single quiet reading room. (p. 70)

It is only logical to conclude that, as most library budgets are fixed and must include major expenditures for audio books, videos, software, CD-ROMs, and maintenance of expensive computer equipment, expenditures for print materials must decline.

Activities for the Classroom

At this point, it might seem paradoxical to suggest that the most effective way a teacher can keep the printed word alive in the classroom is to utilize a multimedia, multisensory approach to language study, but that is precisely what I advocate. It is up to the teacher to find creative, challenging ways that the nonprint media can foster students' linguistic development. Integrating electronic media into a curriculum dependent on human interaction with black print on a white page may provide students, who might otherwise eschew print, with opportunities to read, write, and speak words in a variety of media—film, video, television, CD-ROM, the Internet, music, and e-mail, as well as books. Following, I offer five different activities that attempt to revitalize the rich experience of language through electronic media.

1. The audio-visual poem (individual, pairs, or groups)
   a. Play a piece of music that has appeared in a number of films, commercials, and television shows. (Vivaldi's *The Four Seasons* and Barber's *Adagio for Strings* seem to be very popular with advertisers and filmmakers.)
   b. Students write down whatever ideas and images the music brings up for them.

c. Students choose a format for their poem from a specified list of three to five poetic forms—haiku, limerick, sonnet, or pantoum, for example. (It is best to have sample poems and step-by-step instructions for how to construct a poem in the various formats.) Sometimes I use examples from *The Handbook of Poetic Forms* (Padgett, 1987).

d. Students transfer their writing into the poetic forms of their choice.

e. Ask students to recite their poems to a close friend or a member of the family. Students should ask the friend what kind of music or pictures would go with the poem. Students should record the input from friends, but should accept or reject the advice at their own discretion.

f. Students create an audio or video collage to accompany their new poems using commercially available videos, music, or images or text from the Internet.

g. Students read their poems aloud to the class, accompanied by the audio or video collage (which may be on audiotape, videotape, or videodisc).

h. If the school has a video editing machine, a student could compile audio or video, images or text from the Internet and the recitation of the poem onto a single videocassette.

i. Furnish students with additional advertisements, films, or television shows that have used the piece of music (or give students ongoing credit for collecting them).

2. The Shakespeare rip-off song (individual, pairs, or groups)

a. Students write the lyrics of a favorite song or nursery rhyme, or they compose an original song themselves. Students may be encouraged to select especially simplistic or childish songs, though a serious poem will also do nicely.

b. On another sheet of paper, students try to translate as many words of the song or poem as they can into more sophisticated, Shakespearean language. For purposes of this exercise, it sometimes is interesting to allow students to dramatically alter the tone and themes of the original piece.

c. Once the rough translation is completed, ask students to look for opportunities to use ellipsis and to reduce repetition (unless the repetition is intended, of course). Peer edit, if desired.

d. Before the performance of their songs, students should hand out their "Shakespearean rip-off" lyrics.

e. Students either record the new poem or song on cassette and play it in front of the class or perform it live. Encourage students with musical ability to use music in their presentations (newly created music or an adaptation of the original).

f. Peers attempt to guess the original work and vote for their favorite presentation. (This activity also works well using comic strips from the newspaper or television advertisements instead of song lyrics.)

3. Transforming the vocabulary worksheet into a multimedia experience (pairs)

a. Place students in pairs.

b. Give each pair of students the responsibility for one vocabulary word.

c. Give students 10 minutes to illustrate their word. Students may draw, cut out pictures in magazines, use computer clip art, or use images from the Internet. After the images have been selected (printed and cut out), students should paste them on a large piece of posterboard and beside it write their own brief definition in large letters. Encourage students to use mnemonic devices.

d. Have the students explain their posters, then perform a live 30-second skit that illustrates the meaning of their word.

e. Give an extra point on the next vocabulary test to the first student each day to use one of the vocabulary words in class in "everyday conversation."

f. If more than one class has the same vocabulary words, place all the posterboards with the same words in the same area. Hang the posterboards conspicuously around the room until the exam is given.

4. Vocabulary chain e-mail letters or telephone calls (individual or group)

a. Create a flowchart with PowerPoint, Persuasion, or another presentation software package. If you do not have access to these, use a ruler. Draw a flowchart in which one green box is at the top, five red boxes are under the top green box, and five more blue boxes are under each of the red boxes. This is a flowchart for 31 students that is easily modifiable for more or fewer students.

b. Give the student whose name is in the top green box the vocabulary list a day before you hand it out to the rest of the class. The student should write definitions of the words, be able to pronounce them correctly, and use them in a sentence.

c. The next day, speak individually with the student whose name is in the top green box. Answer any questions he or she might have about the vocabulary. Then, hand out the list of vocabulary words to the rest of the class.

d. A day or two before the vocabulary test, the student whose name is in the top green box e-mails or calls the students whose names appear in the five red boxes and helps them review for the vocabulary test. Then, each of the students whose names appear in the five red boxes e-mails or calls each of the students whose names appear in the five blue boxes. By the day of the exam, everyone in class has received an e-mail message or a telephone call and has reviewed for the exam.

e. Shift responsibilities weekly. At the end of the term, give a prize to the individual whose name was in the top green box when the class scored the highest on the exam.

5. The secret language police (individual or pairs)

a. Designate two students in class to serve as the secret language police.

b. The secret language police have the job of communicating the words and definitions of two bonus vocabulary words to other members of class.

c. The secret language police cannot directly state, "These are the bonus words and they mean...," but they should use the words in their own comments during class.

d. The secret language police are encouraged to spread the words around to the principal and to other teachers.

e. If the secret language police convince the principal (or whoever makes the school announcements) to use their words over the public address system, they receive five extra points on the exam of their choice. If they spot one of their words in a newspaper, magazine, book, or Web site and highlight it for the class before the day of the exam, they receive another five points.

Conclusions

You can keep an old tradition going only by renewing it in terms of current circumstances. (Campbell & Moyers, 1988, p. 21)

The United States, unlike countries such as France or Iceland, has no institution to look after the language, no one to nurture its development or cultivate a respect for its heritage. The accessibility and comprehensibility of the image, the proliferation of new technologies, the focus of current reforms in education, the influence of advertising, and the nature of language used in nonprint media all have contributed to the decline of the word. In many ways, books have remained viable only as a member of the product line in a multipronged, carefully choreographed marketing plan.

When the executive branch of the U.S. government pledges billions of dollars to give schools Internet access, when a U.S. phone company promises to donate funds to help establish a communications infrastructure for every elementary and secondary school in the United States, and when international computer manufacturers announce that they are going to begin aggressively pursuing educational endeavors, teachers can be certain that the escalation of electronically mediated technologies in schools will continue unabated into the future.

Although technology could be a powerful ally in teaching, too often the "bells and whistles" drive the curriculum, not the teacher. If the written word is to survive, it will not be because a group of teachers have chosen to stop using their computers or televisions, but because they have managed to weld language to the electronic media. When a teacher shifts the emphasis from a machine's capabilities to the individual he or she greets every day in the classroom, then technology becomes another tool to enhance learning. Ideally, after a teacher decides on the goals for a classroom, then he or she can begin thinking about how current technologies might be used to help students achieve the goals.

Words are the soul of teaching literature, drama, and composition. Ideally, teachers should use technology as a tool to promote mastery of the language rather than allow the technological marvel of the moment to dictate what happens next.

References

Anderson, J., & Anderson, B. (1993). The myth of persistence of vision revisited. *Journal of Film and Video*, *45*(1), 3–12.

Baines, L. (1996). From page to screen: When a novel is interpreted for film, what gets lost in the translation? *Journal of Adolescent & Adult Literacy*, *39*(8), 612–622.

Baines, L. (1997a). Dispensing with intellect. *Journal of Adolescent & Adult Literacy*, *40*(5), 385–386,

Baines, L. (1997b). Future schlock. *Phi Delta Kappan*, *78*(7) 493–498.

Baines, L. (1997c). Film, video, and books: Some considerations for learning and teaching. In J. Flood, S. Heath, & D. Lapp (Eds.), *A handbook for literacy educators: Research on the communicative and visual arts* (pp. 545–557). New York: Macmillan.

Baker, N. (1996, October 14). The author vs. the library. *The New Yorker*, 50–63.

Bandura, A. (1968). What TV violence can do to your child. In O. Larsen (Ed.), *Violence and the mass media* (pp. 50–75). New York: Harper & Row.

Birkerts, S. (1990). *An artificial wilderness*. Boston, MA: David Godine.

Birkerts, S. (1994). *The Gutenberg elegies*. New York: Fawcett Columbine.

Boorstin, D. (1962). *The image*. New York: Harper & Row.

Boyle, T.C. (1996). In A. Neubauer, Can fiction writing still be taught? *Poets & Writers Magazine* (pp. 42–53).

Boysen, T. (1996, February 21). The governors and their Stone Age schools. *Education Week*, 56.

Burroughs, (1989). In G. Plimpton (Ed.), *The writer's chapbook*. New York: Viking.

Campbell, J., & Moyers, B. (1988). *The power of myth*. New York: Doubleday.

Canary, D., & Spitzberg, B. (1993). Loneliness and media gratifications. *Communications Research, 20*(6), 800–821.

Cantor, J. (1991). Fright responses to mass media productions. In J. Bryant & D. Zillmann (Eds.), *Responding to the screen* (pp. 169–197). Hillsdale, NJ: Erlbaum.

Cantor, J., & Reilly, S. (1982). Adolescents' fright reactions to television and films. *Journal of Communication, 32*(1), 87–99.

Chism, O. (1994). Electronic publishing bids to revolutionize the U.S. book industry. *The Dallas Morning News*, 37A.

Clark, R. (1983). Reconsidering research on learning from media. *Review of Educational Research, 53*, 445–459.

Clark, R. (1985). Confounding in educational computing research. *Journal of Educational Computing Research, 1*(2), 28–42.

Clark, R. (1991). When researchers swim upstream: Reflections on an unpopular argument about learning from media. *Educational Technology, 31*(2), 34–38.

Clark, R. (1994). Media will never influence learning. *Educational Technology Research and Development, 42*(2), 21–29.

Cross, C.(1989). The influence of a positive portrayal of specific elderly individuals in a film series on the cognitive, effective, and behavioral components of children's attitudes toward the elderly (Doctoral dissertation, The University of Maryland, 1989). *Dissertation Abstracts International, 50*, 3799A.

Csikszentmihalyi, M. (1984). *Flow*. New York: HarperCollins.

Csikszentmihalyi, M. (1993). *The evolving self*. New York: Harper Perennial.

Csikszentmihalyi, M. (1996). Education for the twenty-first century. *Daedalus, 124,* 107–114.

Csikszentmihalyi, M., & Larsen, R. (1986). *Being adolescent.* New York: Basic Books.

Csikszentmihalyi, M., Rathunde, K., & Whalen, S. (1993). *Talented teenagers.* New York: Cambridge University Press.

Cutlip, S. (1995). *Public relations history.* Hillsdale, NJ: Erlbaum.

DeLoughry, T. (1996). Reaching a critical mass. *The Chronicle of Higher Education,* pp. A17–20.

Dimsmore, C. (1937). *The great poets and the meaning of life.* Boston, MA: Houghton Mifflin.

Douglas, W., & Olson, B. (1996). Subversion of the American family? *Communications Research, 23*(1), 73–99.

Eisenman, R., Girdner, E., Burroughs, R., & Routman, M. (1993). *Adolescence, 28*(111), 527–532.

Englehardt. T. (1991). Reading may be harmful to your kids: In the Nadirland of today's children's books. *Harper's, 282*(1693), 55–62.

Fernandez, E. (1993, January 22–24). TV vs. books. *USA Weekend,* p. 8.

Franzen, J. (1996). Perchance to dream: In the age of images, a reason to write novels. *Harper's, 292*(1751), 35–54.

Gardner, H. (1983). *Frames of mind: The theory of multiple intelligences.* New York: Basic Books.

Gardner, H. (1993). *Multiple intelligences.* New York: Basic Books.

Hansen, C., & Krygowski, W. (1994, February). Arousal-augmented priming effects: Rock music videos and sex object schemas. *Communication Research,* 24–47.

Herog, J., & Far, D. (1995, October). The impact of press coverage on social beliefs: The case of HIV transmission. *Communications Research,* 545–574.

Kernan, A. (1990). *The death of literature.* New Haven, CT: Yale Press.

Kosslyn, S., Thompson, W., Kim, I., & Alpert, N. (1995, November 30). Topographical representations of mental images in the primary visual cortex. *Nature,* 496–498.

Krystal, A. (1996, March). Closing the books: A once devoted reader arrives at the end of the story. *Harper's, 292*(1750), 54–60.

Limbreglia, R., & Bernhardt, K. (1995). *A Jack Kerouac romnibus.* New York: Penguin Electronic.

Linz, D. (1989). Exposure to sexually explicit materials and attitudes toward rape. *Journal of Sex Research, 26*(1), 50–84.

Oliver, M. (1993, February). Adolescents' enjoyment of graphic horror. *Communication Research, 20*(1), 30–50.

Ong, W. (1967). *The presence of the word.* New Haven, CT: Yale Press.

Ong, W. (1982). *Orality and literacy.* New Haven, CT: Yale Press.

Padgett, R. (1987). *The handbook of poetic forms.* New York: Teachers & Writers Collaborative.

Peck, K., & Dorricott, D. (1994). Why use technology? *Educational Leadership, 51*(7), 11–14.

Postman, N. (1992). *Technopoly.* New York: Knopf.

Postman, N. (1995). *The end of education.* New York: Knopf.

Quality Education Data. (1996). *Technology in the schools.* Denver, CO: Author.

Roberts, P. (1996, June). Virtual Grub Street. *Harper's, 292*(1753), 71–77.

Rock, H., & Cummings, A. (1994). Can videodiscs improve student outcomes? *Educational Leadership, 51*(7), 46–50.

Rubin, A. (1993). Audience activity and media use. *Communication Monographs, 60*(1), 98–105.

Sarafino, E. (1986). *The fears of childhood.* New York: Human Sciences Press.

Scholle, D. (1991). Reading the audience, reading resistance: Prospects and problems. *Journal of Film and Video, 43,* 80–89.

Shrum, L.J. (1995, August). Assessing the social influence of television. *Communications Research,* 402–429.

Singal, D. (1991, November). The other crisis in American education. *Atlantic Monthly,* pp. 59–74.

Stauber, J., & Rampton, S. (1996). *Toxic sludge is good for you.* New York: Common Courage Press.

Steiner, G. (1984). *George Steiner: A reader.* New York: Oxford University Press.

Stine, R.L. (1995). *The Cataluna chronicles: The deadly fire.* New York: Pocket Books.

Stoll, C. (1995). *Silicon snake oil.* New York: Doubleday.

Thornburg, D. (1989, March). Learning Curve. *A+ Magazine,* 191–194.

Tisdale, S. (1997, March). Silence, please: The public library as entertainment center. *Harper's, 294*(1762), 65–74.

Wepner, S., Seminoff, N., & Blanchard, J. (1996, February/March). On screen books of the 90s. *Reading Today, 13*(4), 28.

West, D. (1995, September 25). The horror of R.L. Stine. *The Weekly Standard,* 43–46.

Williams, B. (1996). *The World Wide Web for teachers.* Foster City, CA: IDM Books.

Williams, T. (1989). In G. Plimpton (Ed.), *The writer's chapbook.* New York: Viking.

AUTHOR INDEX

SUBJECT INDEX

Note: Page references followed by *f* indicate figures.